Meeting the Challenge of HIV Infection in Family Foster Care

Constance M. Ryan, Chair
CWLA Task Force on Children and HIV Infection,
Subcommittee on Family Foster Care
and
L. Jean Emery
CWLA HIV/AIDS Program Director
Senior Program Consultant

Child Welfare League of America
Washington, DC

CHILD WELFARE LEAGUE OF AMERICA, INC.

440 First Street, NW, Suite 310, Washington, DC 20001-2085

CURRENT PRINTING (last digit)

10 9 8 7 6 5 4 3 2 1

Cover design by Jennifer Riggs
Text design by Eve Malakoff-Klein

Printed in the United States of America

ISBN # 0–87868–440–9

CONTENTS

PREFACE

The child welfare field has been facing increasing demands in the delivery of family foster care services. In response to the immense challenges facing the family foster care system as we enter the '90s, in January, 1990, the Child Welfare League of America (CWLA) and the National Foster Parent Association (NFPA) launched the first family foster care commission, comprising pre-eminent representatives of the foster care field, agency executives, foster parents, political leaders, and members of academia. Its agenda was to define family foster care for the 1990s and lay the groundwork for the creation of model programs across the country. This important new initiative was prompted by the most complicated problems ever to confront family foster care.

Medically fragile children needing out-of-home care include those with HIV infection. Projections of the number of children with HIV infection and/or AIDS continue to vary considerably. HIV serosurveys of blood specimens from newborn infants, collected by the Center for Disease Control (CDC), indicate that 1,500 to 2,000 HIV-positive infants were born in 1989 [*MMWR* November 30,1990]. CDC projects a cumulative total of 11,000 to14,000 children with HIV infection by 1993. Dr. James Oleske of Children's Hospital in Newark, New Jersey, put forth in 1989 an estimate of 10,000 to 20,000 symptomatic HIV-infected children by 1991. Admiral James Watkins, former chair of the Presidential Commission on the Human Immunodeficiency Virus Epidemic, predicted in 1988 that the number of children and adolescents infected with HIV would reach 20,000 by 1991 [Report of the Commission 1988], with 57% of this group under the age of six.

The Pediatric AIDS Coalition, which comprises 21 national organizations including CWLA, and advocates for children, youths, and families whose lives are affected by HIV infection and AIDS, offers the following statistical analysis in its 1990 legislative agenda:

> The rate of increase in reported cases of AIDS among children under the age of 13 was 53.7% from 1988-1989. AIDS will be the fifth leading cause of death for all children in the next decade, and a major cause of mental retardation.

> More than 81% of young children with AIDS are born to parents who are infected or at risk of infection due to drug use or sexual contacts. This indicates the important role that women of childbearing years play in the epidemic. Together, the 11,922 reported cases of AIDS among women and children represent more than 10% of all cases. In New Jersey, they represent nearly 25%. [Pediatric AIDS Coalition Legislative Agenda 1990]

A recent study in a major epicenter city projected that between 52,000 and 72,000 children (not necessarily infected with HIV themselves) will be orphaned and in need of care as a result of their parents' death from AIDS [Norwood 1989]. Because a number of these children will need foster care placement, extra attention must be given to special training for foster parents and staff members and careful decisions must be made about the difficult issues that accompany the presence of HIV infection, such as testing, confidentiality, and discrimination.

Concern over the projections about a growing number of children with HIV infection was embodied in a resolution of the CWLA 1990 Biennial Assembly to help guide the field for the next two years. Resolution 11 states: "That CWLA and its member agencies implement the use of current information and/or training in HIV infection for casework staff, kinship care and foster care families, supervisors, administrators, and board members."

Under the leadership of Chair Constance Ryan, Coordinator of the Medical Unit of New Jersey's Division of Youth and Family Services, the Subcommittee on Family Foster Care and HIV/AIDS, a working group representing the CWLA membership and the CWLA Task Force on Children and HIV Infection, has indeed performed an important service to the field by developing this publication to guide child welfare agencies in giving more complete and compassionate services to children, youths, and their families who are affected by HIV/AIDS. Vice Chair Ben Eide, Children's Home Society of Washington/founding member of the CWLA Task Force on Children and HIV Infection, and the other members of the subcommittee (see Appendix A) deserve our gratitude for the diligence, expertise, and intelligence they brought to this effort, and the speed with which they prepared it for the field.

David S. Liederman
Executive Director
Child Welfare League of America
Washington, DC

INTRODUCTION

Child welfare practitioners have always worked with the most vulnerable children, youths, and families. Poverty, child abuse, substance abuse, homelessness, and lack of adequate prenatal and follow-up health care for the disadvantaged and disenfranchised are not new problems to the system or its professionals. Today the cumulative effects of these conditions are having a powerful and pervasive impact on overall public health and on child welfare service delivery. The escalating number of infants exposed in utero to the effects of drugs, particularly crack cocaine, is giving rise to a whole new population of medically fragile children. The long-term chronic effects of this exposure are as yet unknown. HIV infection, with its interrelatedness to poverty, homelessness, and drug and alcohol abuse, adds a new seriousness to an already grave picture.

Across the nation, HIV infection wears different faces, and different stages of the epidemic can be seen. Some communities are already immersed in action, some are looking ahead and planning, and some are still saying "Not here." For child welfare, HIV infection most often wears the face of a child, an adolescent, or a mother. We cannot ignore the epidemiology of the disease, which has clearly demonstrated a shift from homosexual to heterosexual transmission, from infected men to women, and from women to children.

June Osborne, Chair of the National Commission on the Acquired Immune Deficiency Syndrome, reports [1990]: "If one watches U.S. trends, women are the fastest growing component of the HIV epidemic; male to female ratios of infected people have been dropping steadily so that they are 3:1 in numerous national surveys, compared to 11:1 a few years ago, and are nearing 1:1 in areas where the virus has been around the longest."

Serving children and families affected by HIV poses some of child welfare's greatest challenges. HIV infection does, however, throw a highly concentrated light on the deficits in the system. It also thrusts the child welfare system into what is perceived to be unfamiliar territory, where attention is focused on the disease and its medical complexities. HIV infection/AIDS is both a medical and a social problem. One cannot deal with it without dealing with the problems of poverty, homelessness, and substance abuse. Nowhere is this more evident than in the families served by child welfare agencies. For this reason, close collaboration between child welfare and health care professionals is imperative in all aspects of prevention, planning, policy development, intervention, and advocacy.

Ironically, HIV infection has also brought forth the best in the system, most poignantly in the family foster care response. Family foster care, in the absence of the biological parent or extended family, has once again tried to fill the void by providing a loving, consistent, supportive, homelike environment for these chronically ill children.

A wide range of developmental, health, and social services is required, particularly if the lives of children and their families are to be enhanced. Experience with family foster care for infants and children who are HIV infected has proven that the caring, affectionate, consistent attention possible in specialized family foster care may be a key ingredient in a successful and coordinated, community-based approach that will benefit the health of children and extend their life span beyond what medical care in a hospital environment alone can do. A successful system of care, therefore, must consider the coordination of social services and medical care, including financial supports, in order to assure the continuing participation of the family.

Osborne [1990] observed: "The only new thing about AIDS is the virus itself. Neither the philosophical dilemmas, the human inequities, the financing challenges, nor the legal, ethical and medical quandaries exposed by the disease are particular to AIDS." And so it is with child welfare. Whether we live in a geographic area with a high incidence of infection or one with a low incidence, the best practice principles accepted for working with children and families are applicable to those affected by HIV.

> The concentration of AIDS cases in children in New York, New Jersey and Florida has lessened over the last few years. This is not an indication that their numbers have decreased or that their problems have eased, but instead is an indication that other states/cities are experiencing growing numbers and will soon have to deal with the same problems New York, Newark, and Miami have faced. [Macro Systems 1988]

In 1990 the number of infants and children under the age of 13 reported as AIDS cases had reached 2,525 [Centers for Disease Control August 1990] and was growing steadily every month. As of the same date, 568 adolescents (age 13 to 19) were reported in the United States as having AIDS.

Many children and adolescents may be HIV positive and either asymptomatic or only mildly symptomatic, and therefore not included in the CDC count. The reported cases particularly understate the problem with respect to adolescents. Twenty percent of the diagnosed AIDS cases in the United States—29,609 cases—have occurred in the age grouping of 20 to 29, according to the 1990 CDC report. Since AIDS may have an incubation period of up to 10 years from the time of infection to symptomatic AIDS, it is agreed that a high proportion of this adult group became infected with HIV in their teen years.

HIV infection is a chronic condition. Those infected by it have an unknown life expectancy. Many demands will be placed on a foster family's personal, social, and financial resources when caring for a child with HIV infection, especially when the biological family is also involved. The unpredictable course of the disease and the fact that AIDS is still a terminal chronic illness are not the least of the elements that must be dealt with in the selection, training, and preparation of foster families. Child welfare agencies must plan to support these families intensively and compassionately, beginning with preparation for fostering, on through the placement, and continuing after the death of a child.

This publication is based upon current medical knowledge of, and legal requirements related to, HIV infection. More importantly, it integrates these requirements with sound child welfare practice. At times, law and child welfare practice may be at odds. Where the law appears to impede the provision of coordinated, child-centered, family-focused, community-based services, child welfare agencies must advocate for reform.

This document is intended as a guide to the components necessary for developing a family foster care response to HIV infection. It is a supplement to, but does not replace, CWLA's two previous guides for recommended practice: *Report of the CWLA Task Force on Children and HIV Infection: Initial Guidelines;* and *Serving HIV-Infected Children, Youth, and Their Families: A Guide for Residential Group Care Providers.* In addition, it sets forth an agenda for advocacy and future challenges.

These guidelines are predicated on the following premises: (1) that HIV infection is both a medical and a social problem, and requires specialized services that demand a high level of expertise and knowledge; (2) that the disease must be demystified for staff members, caregivers, and the community by means of education and case-by-case consultation; (3) that treatment of the child must be within the context of the family, however that family is defined; (4) that service delivery for the child must be designed to maintain and strengthen the family unit and must be child-centered, family-focused, and community-based; and (5) that care must be coordinated to the multifaceted needs of both the child and the family, and public, voluntary, and volunteer agencies must work together toward that end.

Throughout this document the reader will notice various case examples. These vignettes are composites of actual cases encountered by the subcommittee members. They represent the critical issues most frequently faced by child welfare practitioners and hopefully illustrate further the concepts these guidelines are stressing.

In conclusion, I wish to express my sincere appreciation to all the subcommittee participants for their tireless efforts and willingness to struggle with the complexities and challenges that presented themselves throughout the development of these guidelines.

Constance M. Ryan
Chair, CWLA Task Force on Children with HIV Infection
Family Foster Care Subcommittee
Coordinator, Medical Unit
State of New Jersey
Division of Youth and Family Services
Trenton, NJ

Beyond Medical Intervention: The Power of Family Foster Care

Virginia Anderson, M.D.

It is the ultimate goal of all health, social, and educational services for children to ensure that children develop to optimal levels. Chronically ill children must grow toward independence, develop positive self-images, and learn to manage and control as many aspects of their illness as possible. The medical model alone, however, cannot ensure this progression. These children need both medical treatment and technology and nurturing within a family home environment by compassionate, informed individuals who are consistently devoted to children's physical and psychosocial needs. Children with HIV infection and AIDS have a chronic progressive disease punctuated by acute episodes of illness, including common childhood infections, diarrhea, weight loss, and pneumonia. With treatment, children often recover enough to return to their usual daily activities.

To talk about AIDS in children, one needs to talk about families, particularly women: The majority of HIV/AIDS cases in children are related to perinatal transmission. Nationally, in 1984, about 7% of all adult and adolescent cases reported to the CDC were female; as of August 31, 1990, 10% were female. One of the risk behaviors most frequently linked to perinatal transmission of HIV infection is maternal substance abuse. Nationally, as of August 31, 1990, the exposure category for 51% of adult and adolescent females reported was intravenous drug use; for 32% it was heterosexual contact.

Services are needed for all at-risk or infected women, regardless of their reproductive capacity. Appropriate services for all at-risk women could empower them to practice safer sex or discontinue their drug use. Pregnant women who are at risk, or who are HIV positive, even if asymptomatic, require special resources. Many at-risk women already have inadequate access to prenatal care. The health threat that HIV infection poses to pregnant women cannot be overlooked. All of these considerations point to the importance of thoughtful counseling of at-risk women who are, or desire to become, pregnant.

Women, and especially mothers, frequently ignore their own health care while attending to their child's needs, particularly if the child is also infected with HIV. Consequently, women delay treatment until the disease has progressed to the point where they are no longer able to care for a chronically ill child alone. If this woman happens to be a mother without a critical support system, the child is often referred for foster placement.

Whether the child with HIV infection is cared for in his or her own home, in a kinship home, or in a family foster home, the power and strength of a permanent, stable, nurturing, and loving environment is apparent. The home setting allows for treatment of the disease as well as optimal development of the child. Children with HIV infection who are abandoned in the hospital will have a shorter life span than those placed with caring families. A loving home environment can prolong the length and enhance the quality and meaning of the child's life as much as the administration of anti-AIDS drugs. This environment will allow children's potential to be maximized despite their disabilities. Self-acceptance and social integration should be emphasized.

Care for chronically ill children should be coordinated, community-based, and both child-centered and family-focused.

> Coordinated care means that members of a multidisciplinary team (MDT), focused on a child's well-being, must communicate and integrate their expertise to conserve resources, avoid conflict, and ensure that multiple needs are met, usually under the guidance of a social worker and/or nurse case manager, with medical supervision by a primary care pediatrician.

> Community-based resources reduce travel time, provide a sense of belonging someplace, encourage relationships, and increase the likelihood of ongoing participation in, and compliance with, a program of care.

> Child-centered, family-focused care encompasses the needs of family members and monitors the effect of chronic illness on well siblings. Protection of family integrity includes respect for family values, support, and openness to innovative approaches such as enlisting co-parents, foster grandparents, or other surrogates who can provide loving care or

respite. Family-oriented case managers must use ingenuity, concrete services, and open communication to keep families intact as long as feasible. Each child needs a program that enables her or him to measure progress and bolster self-esteem.

Physically challenged children must be offered the possibility to reach, grow, learn, and transcend their disabilities. Self-acceptance and opportunities to play and enjoy the company of peers are critical for social development. HIV infection is more than a disease. It is a state of being that makes its impact felt on all aspects of living and must be faced on multiple levels. Societal attitudes and personal beliefs must accommodate and embrace those infected so as to optimize development against a background of intermittent illness.

Expectations may have to be modified, and planning must be flexible. Living with AIDS is filled with especially meaningful moments, uncertainty, and hope, interspersed with anger, all of which can be tolerated and cared for in a nurturing family. Medical care is not enough. A loving environment may prolong the lives of some children and certainly will enhance life for every terminally ill child. Family and group counseling must be available for all children with HIV infection or AIDS, their caregivers, and their siblings. Listening to the children and their families will achieve the best-coordinated response to a multiplicity of problems.

FREQUENTLY ASKED MEDICAL QUESTIONS

Pediatric HIV infection is a complex disease that has many implications for family foster care agencies and foster parents. An understanding of the disease process helps in planning and caring for children affected by HIV. This series of questions was developed by members of the subcommittee as representative of those most commonly asked by family foster care parents and providers. The answers were prepared from material used in the training of family foster care providers by the National Pediatrics HIV Resource Center, Carolyn Burr, Coordinator.

What is HIV? How does it cause disease? What are its symptoms?

The Human Immunodeficiency Virus (HIV) is a retrovirus that integrates with the DNA of human cells. HIV infects specialized white blood cells called T-helper cells or T4 cells. These cells play a critical role in the body's immune system.

As the HIV grows and reproduces in T4 cells, the cells are destroyed. The body then has difficulty fighting off infections and regulating its immune system. Opportunistic infections, like pneumocystis carinii pneumonia (PCP), do not occur in persons with a healthy immune system, but occur frequently in persons with seriously compromised immune systems, such as those with AIDS. A child with HIV often has extremely high levels of immunoglobulins (antibodies) that are not functional and do not protect the child against disease. He or she is susceptible to serious bacterial infections such as meningitis and sepsis (bacteria in the blood), as well as other common childhood infections like chronic otitis media (ear infections) and skin infections.

Children with HIV have many nonspecific symptoms, such as enlarged lymph nodes, enlarged liver and spleen, oral thrush, diarrhea, weight loss, and fever. A lung disease called lymphocytic interstitial pneumonia (LIP) is a common finding in children with HIV. Over time, LIP causes a child's blood to be poorly oxygenated.

HIV may attack the brain directly, resulting in failure to achieve developmental tasks or a loss of developmental milestones already achieved, loss of motor function, decreased intellectual skills, loss of self-care abilities, and behavioral changes. Neurological changes can be the first symptoms of HIV or can occur later in the illness.

HIV causes damage to many organs, leading to heart problems, kidney disease, hepatitis, and other conditions. Cancer also can occur because of the damage HIV has done to the immune system. HIV is a deadly and dangerous virus. It can damage almost all body systems of the infected child.

How is HIV transmitted, particularly to children?

Human Immunodeficiency Virus (HIV), the virus that causes AIDS, is transmitted through contact with infected blood, semen, or vaginal fluids, or from mother to infant during pregnancy, in childbirth, and in rare cases, through breast milk. Of the children under age 13 with HIV who have been identified through the United States Centers for Disease Control (CDC) AIDS surveillance as of August 31, 1990, 10% were exposed to HIV-infected blood through blood transfusion or blood products. Eighty percent had a parent with HIV infection or at risk for HIV.

What does it mean that a child is HIV positive?

It means that when tested, a child's blood contained antibodies produced by the body because of the presence of HIV. A positive HIV test for a particular child must be interpreted in relation to the age of the child.

An infant born to a mother with HIV infection may or may not be infected with the virus. The infant receives the mother's antibodies in utero or during birth, and will test positive for HIV antibodies at birth, and possibly up to 24 months after birth, on the common screening tests for HIV antibody (ELISA and Western Blot). Data from current studies of infants born to mothers with HIV infection indicate that between 25% and 40% of the infants will actually be infected with HIV [Connor et al. 1989]. The other 60% to 75% of the infants are not infected with HIV and will lose their mothers' HIV antibodies. New tests currently being developed may make it possible to identify an infant's HIV status with greater certainty.

Children over age 24 months who are identified as HIV antibody positive by ELISA and Western Blot tests are considered to be HIV infected. These older children can also be diagnosed as HIV infected if they show symptoms that meet the CDC case definition of AIDS or if the virus is cultured from blood or tissues [CDC, MMWR 1987]. (See Appendix C.)

The reliability of HIV antibody test results for older children and adolescents is comparable to that for adults. A negative HIV antibody result is a good indication that the person is not HIV infected. An individual who engages in risk activities in certain circumstances, however, may test negative for antibodies and yet be HIV infected, as for example in very early infection.

Antibody tests for HIV in children can be difficult to interpret. Evaluation of children for HIV infection should be done by health professionals who are knowledgeable about pediatric HIV infection.

Why will I not know for certain the infection status of an infant who tests HIV positive?

As previously noted, the potential presence of maternal antibodies in an infant less than 24 months old makes the determination of HIV status difficult. The presence of maternal antibodies in the infant's blood results in a positive HIV antibody test. New technologies for diagnosing HIV, currently being developed, should prove helpful in solving this problem as they become available. They may not be available in all areas, however, or may be available for investigational use but not approved for clinical diagnostic use.

Viral culture of HIV, in which the virus actually is grown from blood or tissue, is available in some centers. At present the technique is expensive and laborious [Falloon et al. 1989]. It can identify the virus if it is present; a negative result, however, does not rule out the presence of HIV. Tests that detect viral antigen, that is, protein from the virus itself, also are available in some university and commercial laboratories. These tests are simpler and less expensive than viral culture, and will probably become more available as the technology is refined. The PCR, or polymerase chain reaction method, tests white blood cells for the presence of HIV DNA. PCR is a highly specialized technique available in only a few laboratories. The reliability and clinical usefulness of the PCR have not yet been determined.

Each of these diagnostic tests holds the promise of diagnosing HIV infection in infants less than 15 months of age. Until the technologies are refined and their reliability established, however, these tests probably will not be widely available. In general, when infants test positive on viral cultures or viral antigen tests, they are considered to be HIV infected. When infants test negative on viral cultures, viral antigens, or PCR tests, however, their HIV status remains unknown. Negative test results only mean that the virus could not be detected. They cannot rule out the presence of HIV infection.

Interpretation of these tests is complex. Only a physician who is an expert in pediatric HIV should use these tests to evaluate a child. Once the test is carried out, social workers and nurses with appropriate training should counsel the parent, child, or youth about the doctor's interpretation of the test results.

How old must a child or adolescent be before I can be certain of the child's HIV status?

Infants born to a mother who is HIV positive should be tested for HIV antibodies up to two years of age. Physical examination and evaluation of the child's immune status should be performed regularly. Most children who are HIV infected show symptoms of HIV infection that meet CDC criteria for AIDS by age two.

HIV antibody test results in children over two and adolescents are more certain than in younger children. A negative test should be repeated if there is continued exposure to risk of HIV transmission.

If a child, formerly HIV positive, seroconverts to HIV antibody negative, what planning is needed?

Children born to mothers who are HIV positive and who become seronegative by age two should continue to receive routine well-child care and careful monitoring of their health status. Health and social services professionals responsible for the care of such a child should be aware that the child was born to a mother who was HIV positive. Although rare, instances have been reported of children who seroconverted from HIV positive to HIV negative even though they were, in fact, HIV infected [Falloon et al. 1989].

What is the risk of contagion to others when a child has HIV?

The Human Immunodeficiency Virus (HIV) is not spread through casual contact [Rogers et al. 1990]. It can be spread only by direct contact with infected body fluids—blood, semen, vaginal fluids, and in rare cases, breast milk. Although HIV has been found in very small quantities in tears and saliva, there is no evidence that HIV can be transmitted by these fluids. A study by the CDC of families of children with HIV infection found no evidence that HIV could be spread by casual transmission, even to close household contacts.

The use of universal precautions minimizes the risk of exposure to HIV-contaminated fluids. Protective barriers should be used when handling blood or blood-containing material (e.g., bloody diarrhea). (See Appendix E.)

Can the child who is HIV positive spread infectious illnesses to family members or others?

Many of the illnesses for which children who are HIV infected are at risk are opportunistic diseases; that is, they can infect persons whose immune systems function poorly. Children with HIV infection, like all children, can also get infections that could be a risk to others, for example, salmonella. A child with HIV infection may be at increased risk for other infectious diseases as well. Infection control procedures are based on the nature of the disease rather than the child's HIV status. Foster families and foster care agencies should ask their physicians or health providers about specific risks and precautions when any child is diagnosed with an infectious disease. Pulmonary tuberculosis in children, for example, is not considered to be spread by the respiratory route—a contrast to the pattern for tuberculosis in adults. Each infectious disease requires specific management, so specific instructions from medical experts should be sought.

What are the stages in the progression from HIV infection to AIDS?

HIV infection follows a continuum from the asymptomatic stage to full-blown AIDS, with many degrees of wellness and illness in between. The progression of illness varies with each child, but, in general, children with HIV infection become symptomatic at an early age. Of children with AIDS, 50% were diagnosed by one year of age, and 82% by age three [CDC, MMWR 1986]. These children moved rapidly along the continuum of illness to AIDS—the most serious consequence of HIV infection. (See Appendix C for pediatric classification of the disease.) Some children, however, stay healthy longer and may be three or four years of age or older before showing symptoms of HIV infection [Connor 1989]. Individual children progress through the stages at different rates of time for reasons that may be known (such as age of onset or nutritional regimen) or unknown.

The progressive stages of HIV infection in older children and adolescents tend to follow the stages seen in adults with HIV infection, except that persons with hemophilia, infected through transfusion of blood products, have a longer time before development of symptoms.

CDC has charted the following progression of HIV infection in persons over 13 years of age:

Stage 1. *Acute Infection:* Initially infected individuals with HIV. The individual infected may or may not exhibit flu-like symptoms. If present, the symptoms may be so mild as to go unnoticed.

Stage 2. *Asymptomatic Seropositive:* Individual looks well and feels well.

Stage 3. *Persistent Generalized Lymphadenopathy:* Symptomatic infection characterized by generalized lymph node infections.

Stage 4. *Symptomatic Disease:* Severely ill, end stage of HIV infection. Characterized by opportunistic infections that make up the syndrome of AIDS. There are subcategories.

How can a child with HIV infection appear perfectly well?

Children who are HIV infected may be asymptomatic for a period of time and require careful monitoring of their health status. Many of the symptoms of HIV are subtle; parents, foster parents, and those involved in the care of the child should carefully observe his or her health and development. Children with HIV infection should be monitored by health care professionals who are aware of their health history, knowledgeable about pediatric HIV infection, and in contact with other experts in the field. These children should receive the childhood immunizations recommended for HIV-infected children by the CDC [CDC, MMWR 1988]. Their immune status should be monitored at regular intervals to evaluate their T-helper lymphocyte count, immunoglobulin level, and other indicators of immune status. Even children who appear to be asymptomatic can have dramatic, fairly sudden changes in their immune systems that place them at risk for serious infections.

Adolescents and older children who are not infected perinatally tend to follow the adult progression of HIV infection. The incubation period from time of infection to symptomatic illness can be up to ten years or more. Generally this is Stage 2 of the CDC classification in which the person looks well and feels well. Stage 3 can also give the sense of being well and feeling well. Stage 4 (AIDS) is serious, and persons who are HIV infected can have dramatic changes in their physical condition and emotional status from day to day, and particularly in children, from hour to hour.

Preventive therapy with appropriate antibiotics for the most common opportunistic infection, pneumocystis carinii pneumonia (PCP), should be given to children whose immune status is seriously compromised. Illnesses in children with HIV infection must be evaluated quickly and thoroughly by a health professional. Children with HIV are more susceptible than others to serious or fatal infections, and even relatively common infections pose a significant health risk. For example, chicken pox and measles can be serious or fatal infections in the immunocompromised child. A child who is HIV infected and who has been exposed to chicken pox or measles or shows any symptoms of these diseases should be seen immediately by a physician.

Children's growth and development should be carefully followed. Failure to gain weight or to grow can be a serious manifestation of HIV infection. Early and aggressive nutritional intervention can help children live lives of better quality. Evaluation of cognitive and motor development in children with HIV is also critical. Because HIV attacks the brain, failure to achieve appropriate milestones or loss of developmental skills is frequently seen.

As more is learned about pediatric HIV infection, other interventions will be available to children earlier in the course of the disease. Some antiviral therapies, such as AZT, have been approved for children and are currently available. Others are under study. As access to treatment expands, it is important that children of all ages be followed closely through the continuum of illness so they can receive the most current appropriate treatment available. Children may appear healthy because they are at an early stage of infection, are receiving effective medication, or exhibit only subtle signs of illness, but caregivers must remain vigilant.

Why do some children get sick earlier and some later?

The reason some children become symptomatic earlier than others is not yet known. Children with perinatal HIV rarely show symptoms at birth. By CDC criteria, perinatal AIDS is diagnosed at a median age of nine months, while children infected by a blood transfusion are diagnosed with AIDS at a median time interval of 17 months after their transfusion [Rogers et al. 1987]. Some children live a number of years before showing symptoms of HIV infection. The true incubation period for AIDS in children is not yet known.

Pediatric HIV infection is a chronic illness similar to other chronic illnesses such as diabetes or cystic fibrosis. With appropriate supports and care, children with HIV can live for many years and participate in family, school, and community activities.

What kind of symptoms should be monitored in a child with HIV infection?

As noted earlier, foster parents and professionals should be alert for any failure of the child to gain weight or for weight loss, and for any sign of failure to achieve developmental tasks or loss of tasks already achieved. Common physical symptoms include enlarged lymph nodes, oral thrush and candidiasis, diaper rash, fever, diarrhea, and skin rashes. The child's activity level should be carefully observed, since serious infections often show themselves as lethargy or irritability, with or without fever. Foster parents should have access to a consistent health care provider whom they can call at any time or see immediately when they are concerned about the child's health.

What kinds of supportive treatments are available to children with HIV infection?

Good nutrition with nutritional supplements when needed is an important part of caring for children who are HIV infected. Early and aggressive treatment of infections is essential. Developmental evaluations and early intervention programs help monitor and enhance a child's or youth's development. Antibiotics to prevent PCP may be given to a child whose immune function is seriously impaired. Some children are given intravenous gamma globulin (pooled antibodies) to enhance their ability to fight off infection. Children should receive immunizations in accordance with the most current CDC recommendations for children with HIV. These kinds of interventions help children with HIV live healthier lives. The loving attention and nurturing stimulation given by a consistent caregiver are just as crucial as medical care for the physical health of the child, and for the child's mental health.

What antivirals are available for children?

Azidothymidine (AZT), first evaluated on adults with HIV, is now available to children. AZT interferes with the ability of HIV to reproduce in the body, and thus slows progression of the disease.

The process of evaluating the safety and effectiveness of a new drug is slow.

One reason for caution is the creation of side effects. For example, prolonged use of AZT in high doses may cause severe anemia. Individual reactions vary.

Additional drugs are under investigation and may be available to children through the AIDS Clinical Trials Group in the medical centers that participate in investigational drug trials. The location of the center nearest your area and information about any studies currently underway can be found by calling the National Institutes of Health at 1–800–TRIALS–A. Contact with health professionals in your area who are knowledgeable about pediatric HIV is essential. Most departments of pediatrics have specialists in immunology or infectious diseases who may be contacted for referrals.

Agency Policy and Practice

Agency policy must ensure the provision of services to children, youths, and families with HIV infection. Agency policy development is a critical part of preparing to serve these clients. Because HIV/AIDS is a fairly new phenomenon, particularly in the child welfare field, agencies have to become informed about the disease itself; the implications for the care of children and their families who are, or may be, HIV infected; and the laws and regulations that apply. Recommendations for policies that agencies should have in place are outlined in the following sections. They are consistent with the general status of the law at this writing. Since a significant amount of HIV-related law is state- or province-specific, however, agencies should consult with legal counsel in developing agency policy and guidelines. This is particularly important with respect to testing and confidentiality, which are substantially matters of state or provincial law. Furthermore, legal review of HIV-related policies should take place at least biannually or after every legislative session. HIV-related laws are in a state of flux, so agency policies may quickly become outdated.

Coordination and Collaboration

Coordination of social services and medical services is imperative for successful family foster care placement of children with HIV infection. Pediatric HIV infection is a complex disease that requires ongoing partnerships among the child welfare agencies, the health care system, the child, the foster family, and, ideally, the biological family, to provide support and continuity of care. Agencies and foster parents, including kinship caregivers, need access to knowledgeable health care providers who can deliver quality care and answer their medical and health questions. The best interests of the child dictate that the goals, objectives, and functions of the social service and health effort be congruent.

Components of a comprehensive system should include formal, written contracts and agreements and professional networking and resource involvement. Some guidelines for these components follow.

Inter-Agency Coordination and Collaboration

The family foster care agency should develop a collaborative relationship with health care providers and other social service providers and with local support organizations. This relationship helps assure that ongoing care is coordinated and community-based.

The collaboration among health care services, foster care agencies, and foster parents should include:

- Developing linkages with health/medical resources that offer expertise in the care of children with HIV infection, including primary health care, tertiary care/hospitalization services, home health care, developmental services, hospices, and other such services;

- Designating a health care provider known to the foster parent and agency as the contact person within the medical setting for each child;

- Participating as part of the health care team when the child with HIV infection is in the medical setting in order to develop and carry out a plan of care;

- Observing and communicating with each other about the fluctuating medical and health needs of the child and the subsequent need for supports for the foster family.

In addition to working with health care providers, the agency should work with other community agencies to create, coordinate, and deliver services to clients with HIV infection. These community agencies may include social service providers, mental health clinics, organizations serving developmentally disabled clients, community-based AIDS organizations, agencies that serve runaway youths, and juvenile justice agencies, as well as other community groups such as religious organizations and women's groups.

Intra-Agency Coordination

In addition to developing coordination and collaboration among health services, social services, and community resources, the agency should develop a plan or mechanism for coordinating services within the agency itself. The multidisciplinary team (MDT) is a frequently used structure for this type of coordination. The MDT concept is explained fully in two CWLA publications: *Report of the CWLA Task Force on Children and HIV Infection: Initial Guidelines,* and *Serving HIV-Infected Children in Residential Group Care.* The MDT helps the agency set HIV-related policies and procedures, design training, and advocate for services. For individual cases, the team should:

- Review initial intake information, which should include the child's current health status, and select the most appropriate placement for the child;

- Develop an individual treatment plan for the child and family and assign a case manager;

- Review the individual treatment plan regularly and adjust the plan accordingly; and

- Act as final authority in all decision making.

In the child welfare setting, the composition of the MDT varies with the different services the agency delivers and the range of professionals and consultants available to the foster families. For confidentiality reasons, the MDT's makeup may also vary by its activity—that is, individual case consultation vs. setting agency policy and practices. With respect to the latter, where individual clients are not named, the composition of the team may be quite broad and may include agency administrators, board members, social work/clinical consultants, legal counsel, direct service staff members and contractors, school and community agency representatives, and even representatives of agency consumers such as foster parents and biological parents.

When the team is dealing with individual cases, however, its makeup must take into account the restrictions of confidentiality laws and regulations. These requirements vary by state; are often spread out over HIV-specific, child welfare, public health, and licensing statutes; and are all too often ambiguous. As a general rule, however, persons who are not involved in the direct care and treatment of the individual child, or who work for another agency, should not participate in case discussions. The only exceptions might arise when the client or his or her legal surrogate consents to these additional persons; when a state law allows disclosure of HIV information to a person without this consent; or when the team consultation does not identify, directly or indirectly, the client and/or family.

Hospital and medical settings also use multidisciplinary teams for case management of patients. If the child welfare client is under medical care in one of these settings [*CWLA* 1988: 48], a member of the hospital team should be a member of the child welfare multidisciplinary team.

In addition to assembling the multidisciplinary team, the agency has to assure continuity of services and comprehensive care for clients by developing and maintaining contact with the primary care physician or a medical consultant. One case management model promotes community-based care by having primary care physicians work in close consultation with pediatric HIV/AIDS experts in their area or region.

Intake, Assessment, and Placement

Intake and Assessment

The agency must not deny services to a child with HIV infection solely because of that infection. Decisions about placement must never be based solely on the presence of known or suspected HIV infection. Not only would such decisions run counter to the agency's mission of serving children, but they would also be likely to violate federal, state, and provincial antidiscrimination laws. Section 504 of the federal Rehabilitation Act, the more recent Americans with Disabilities Act, and their state law counterparts prohibit denying services or benefits to a handicapped individual (today universally interpreted to include all persons with HIV infection or persons perceived to be infected) if that person is "otherwise qualified" for the service. In other words, services or benefits may be denied only if, for reasons unrelated to the person's HIV status, the person is not qualified for the program. For example, a program that provides family foster care only for infants and young children need not change its admission standards to accommodate an adolescent with HIV infection.

The responsible provision of care should include knowledge of both the psychosocial and physical condition of the client. HIV infection poses a special challenge because of its social, as well as medical, ramifications. An attempt must therefore be made to reconcile potentially conflicting viewpoints: (1) the child's and family's right to privacy; (2) the child's need for early medical intervention if he or she is HIV infected; (3) the child's emotional and social condition if the child becomes labeled and suffers neglect, abuse, or inappropriate or no treatment as a result; and (4) an agency's potential need to know about the medical condition of one of its clients [CWLA 1989: 35].

The skillful gathering of information related to the risk of HIV infection should become standard practice in compiling histories of children, youths, and their families. Knowledge of the risk of HIV infection must become part of everyday awareness, as has knowledge of alcoholism or drug use, and be incorporated into routine history-taking. The best starting point in determining the risk level for a particular infant or young child is a careful assessment of the biological parents.

When taking a history, the worker should first assess the client's knowledge of HIV/AIDS and its risk factors, then provide information that will clarify or correct the client's perceptions as necessary. The next step is to determine from the client whether there are risk factors in the client's history. This two-way information-sharing process is critical to the primary goals of educating about and preventing HIV infection, obtaining early treatment, and providing comprehensive services.

Information to be ascertained from clients should include identification of the following documented risk factors for HIV infection:

- Intravenous (IV) drug use, past or present.

- Unprotected anal, vaginal, or oral intercourse (All risk exposure to infected blood, semen, or vaginal fluid.)

- Sexual activities with many different partners (Multiple exposure increases risk. Individuals who have been involved in using crack cocaine or other mind-altering substances have a higher incidence of HIV infection and other sexually transmitted diseases due to their increased sexual activities.)

- Sexual activities with persons who are, or have been, involved in the risk behaviors delineated above.

It is also essential to find out if individuals belong to any of the following high-risk groups:

- Infants born to known HIV-infected mothers or mothers with risk behaviors.

- Children and youths who have been involuntary sex partners because of sexual assault, rape, and/or sexual abuse.

- Persons with hemophilia, because of their need for blood products. (The current risk to this population, however, has been greatly reduced since the appropriate testing of all blood and blood products was instituted in March 1985.)

- Individuals who received blood transfusions between 1978 and March

1985. (Many older children and adolescents who are HIV positive were infected originally through blood transfusions or from blood products, so it is important to gather any and all information related to blood disorders. Premature infants often receive blood even without surgery or trauma. A question should be asked about this possibility when asking for birth information.)

This information should be gathered carefully, with respect for privacy and confidentiality, because sexual behavior and drug use are sensitive matters.

Corroboration of health information is vital in the assessment process. Obtaining significant health and medical records is essential in helping the multidisciplinary team make an appropriate plan.

Since children with HIV infection have special health needs, agencies should develop well-trained and specialized foster families for these children. The following comprehensive picture of the psychosocial needs of a child with HIV infection, written especially for caregivers, is drawn from *A Practical Guide to Caring for Children with AIDS*, by the New Jersey Department of Human Services, Division of Youth and Family Services [1989]:

> AIDS is a chronic illness. This means the child is frequently ill and medical treatment is constant. The caregiver and the child will spend lots of time with doctors or in hospitals and in ongoing medical care between hospitalizations.
>
> The extent of illness and the intensity of medical treatment will vary with the type of infection. There will be periods when the child is sick but doesn't need hospitalization. For example, the child with a cold or sore throat may be cared for at home with visits to the doctor. An intestinal infection, however, may require hospitalization.
>
> Just as with any other chronic disease, the disease itself and the treatment for the disease can weaken the child physically and emotionally.
>
> For the child with HIV infection, the critical issue is to prevent the disease and its treatment from interfering with the child's development. For the caregiver of a child with HIV infection, the critical issue is to prevent the disease process and its treatment from interfering with family functioning and family interaction with the child.
>
> It is essential to keep the infant and preschool child in the mainstream of family life, so that the child continues to be active, nurtured, and stimulated by family activities. Interacting with the child as you go about

your everyday routine is important to the child's overall development and positive outlook. For the older child, participation in a school program is also critical to development.

The care of any chronically ill person demands lots of energy, patience, and motivation. The physical and emotional demands of caring for a sick child, scheduling and keeping medical appointments, and managing a household can be exhausting. Caregivers need a routine that allows them to be sensitive to the needs of the child and meet their family's needs as well. There must be allowance for such things as quiet time for individuals, privacy for adults, and special time with your other children. Make life as enjoyable as possible for the family.

Placement

There usually is no medical reason for children with HIV infection not to be placed with each other, or with other noninfected children, but mixing populations with special health needs should always be done in consultation with the multidisciplinary team, including the primary care physician.

When the decision has been made to place a child in family foster care, the extensive social, developmental, and medical needs of children who are HIV infected and the resulting physical and emotional stress of caring for a child who is chronically ill must be weighed. This requires pertinent information about the number of children in the foster home, the placement of sibling groups together or in proximity, the protection of the seropositive child from undue exposure to additional infection, and the control of behaviors likely to transmit HIV infection, particularly in sexually active adolescents.

In developing the service plan, the team should adhere to the basic requirement of P.L. 96-272 (the Adoption Assistance and Child Welfare Act), that children be placed in the least restrictive family-like setting, and should undertake the following practices before the child is placed:

- Review the initial assessment of the social, medical, emotional, and educational needs of the child;

- Review the child's current health status and the appropriateness of medical management in regard to accessibility of medical care and responsiveness to the foster family's and the child's needs;

- Assess the strengths of the child and the child's biological family and/or the extended family;

- Review the permanency plan and assess the possibility of the child's return to parents or relatives as caregivers;

- Assess the cultural, racial, and ethnic factors;

- Assess needs, set goals, and determine who is responsible for each goal, how each will be accomplished, and in what time frames;

- Assess the child's potential for participation in investigational medical trials;

- Assess the need for parental consent for possible medical procedures and treatment choices, which may include decisions to test for HIV, participation in medical/clinical trials, stop-treatment decisions, do-not-resuscitate (DNR) orders, and autopsy authorization;

- Identify a primary care physician for ongoing routine medical care;

- Arrange access to ongoing specialized medical care as necessary, and to an array of vital support services as well; and

- Collect all necessary legal documents.

Ideally this plan should be developed before the child is placed, and then assessed every 30 to 90 days after placement. The length of time between reviews may vary in relation to the child's status, that is, his or her health and psychosocial needs. Frequent plan reviews are necessary because that status can change quickly.

Testing, Confidentiality, and Disclosure

Explicit policy statements are required on HIV testing of children, the confidentiality of HIV information, and agency disclosure of a client's HIV status, because agency practice must take into consideration serious legal and clinical implications.

Testing

A four-year-old child who had been sexually abused by a 23-year-old male relative was referred for placement. The relative was a known intravenous drug user and was involved in prostitution. He had been serving as a baby-sitter for this child and three other children in the household under two years of age. The agency's MDT medical consultant recommended that the male relative be tested for HIV

> because of his risk history. Since there was no certainty that
> he actually would be tested, the four year old and the three
> younger children were tested, with repeat testing in six
> months. Counseling was made available to the family.

HIV testing must be carefully considered, and agency policy should clearly articulate the rationale for requesting it. Agency policy should not require mandatory testing of children entering into any of the agency's services, including family foster care. Testing for HIV antibodies must not be used as a means to deny a child placement that the agency can reasonably offer, nor should it be used to provide a rationale for the expulsion or termination of a child from an agency program or setting. A structured intake process is, therefore, vital to reaching an accurate health status assessment as part of a best-practice case plan. This intake procedure may lead to a recommendation, on a case-by-case basis, that the client or prospective client be tested. The test, however, may not be administered without the informed consent of the minor client's parents, or, where legal custody has been transferred by a judicial order, the informed consent of the legal custodian. In some cases, the legal custodian may be the agency. Even here, however, the agency must check state HIV law. Some states, like California, leave consent rights with the parents, even when a child welfare agency has been given legal custody of the child, unless parental rights have been terminated.

Some adolescents may consent to their own health care treatment. Statutes granting this right are often limited to certain circumstances (e.g., mature minors), or to certain kinds of health care (e.g., for sexually transmitted diseases, drug/ alcohol problems). Unless the statute is HIV-specific or has been interpreted to apply to HIV, the application of these statutes to the testing decision may be unclear, and the agency should seek legal counsel. Even if the statute is interpreted to grant consent rights to adolescents, an issue may arise concerning a particular youth's mental competency to consent. The minor may, due to the effects of the HIV infection, or for unrelated reasons, be mentally incompetent. If the agency believes this to be true, it may still have to seek parental permission.

There may be times when parental consent for testing or disclosure of HIV information is legally necessary, but the parent is unavailable or cannot be identified, or when informing the parent of the child's possible health problem could itself be problematic. In such cases the agency could petition a court for permission to test.

Whether it is the parent or the child who consents to testing, the consent must be an informed one. That is, the person must be apprised of any potential adverse consequences of the test. For HIV testing, these may include possible social, health care, economic, housing, job, and other discrimination. The consent should be in writing and specifically for the purpose of giving the HIV test and obtaining the results. This consent is not covered by a general release form granting the agency broad health care decision-making authority, such as may be signed by parents when voluntarily placing their child in foster care. General consents may even be illegal under some state and provincial HIV laws. Many state and provincial public health and child welfare agencies are developing model consent forms for HIV testing and disclosure purposes. Agencies may want to obtain these forms for their own use.

If the HIV antibody testing procedure has not been done before the child's coming to the attention of the agency, any decision about possible testing should be made by the multidisciplinary team. (See the Intake, Assessment, and Placement section above for guidelines pertinent to risk behaviors that may indicate a need for testing.)

Because the responsible provision of appropriate care requires knowledge of the physical condition of the client, testing is sometimes necessary. An agency's decision to advise, request, or conduct testing should be based on written policies that reflect the following considerations:

- Specific reasons for testing related to the well-being of the child or youth;

- Authority to test based upon legal mandates, or the informed consent of the client or those who are legally authorized to make decisions on behalf of the client;

- Access to pre- and post-test counseling within the family foster care agency or its community network;

- A plan for HIV retesting, as necessary;

- Coverage for the cost of pre- and post-test counseling and testing, especially if more expensive follow-up tests are needed (including a plan for children who can consent to testing without parental notification but whose parents have medical insurance);

- Ability to formulate a service plan for seropositive children and their families with the participation of the child's biological parents and/or legal guardian, the foster parents, and (where appropriate) the child;

- Up-to-date knowledge and medical consultation regarding test results and reliability;

- Ability to educate its staff members; and

- A plan for confidential management of test results, whether positive or negative, and other HIV-related information.

Ideally, the results of each test for the child should be explained to the child in an age-appropriate manner and to the biological parents, the legal guardian, the foster parents, and the foster care worker in a way that respects the affectional and legal attachments of all parties involved with the child and the family. In every case, the language for communicating information about HIV test results should be based on the individual's level of understanding about the topic.

It is the responsibility of the multidisciplinary team to make sure that the health care providers do communicate appropriately. It is essential that children who are tested be provided with appropriate pre- and post-test counseling according to their emotional, social, and intellectual level of functioning. Counseling and testing should be obtained at centers with recognized expertise in pediatric HIV infection, not at adult testing sites.

For those who actually receive the test results, decisions regarding who to tell may be limited by state confidentiality laws. In most cases the parent or legal guardian is entitled to this information. The two possible exceptions are cases in which the parent's parental rights have been terminated and those in which the child has consented to the test without parental notification. In the latter situation, laws may vary. In most U.S. states where the child can consent, the parent cannot be notified of the results without the child's permission.

Foster parents are usually entitled to this information under the state HIV confidentiality law. Even where the law is silent or ambiguous, a strong argument, based on federal law and policy, can be made favoring disclosure. As a policy matter, foster parents need information about HIV status to provide proper care of the child. Legally, there is a federal mandate, as part of the 1989 amendments to the Adoption Assistance and Child Welfare Act (P.L. 101-239), that case plans include comprehensive health care information about the child and that "a child's health and education record...is reviewed and updated, and supplied to the foster parent or foster care provider with whom the child is placed..." [42 U.S.C. 675 (as amended)]. Under this law, HIV-related information should be included in the child's case plan and shared with the foster parents.

Prospective adoptive parents, however, may be treated differently. Until the agency is sure that the prospective adoptive parents are interested in and likely to adopt a particular child with HIV, the child's HIV status should not be shared. Some states handle this in their adoption exchanges and directories by indicating that the child has a special medical condition.

Once the agency is satisfied that the prospective adoptive parents are likely to adopt, the child's HIV status should be shared. Without this information the prospective adoptive parents may be foreclosed from seeking adoption subsidies. (Federal subsidies are unavailable if not agreed to before the adoption is legalized.) Furthermore, the agency may eventually be sued by the adoptive parents for not sharing this information. The lawsuit could allege that had the agency informed the prospective adoptive parents of the child's HIV status, they would not have adopted. Medical and other expenses that arise as a result of the child's health problems may therefore be deemed damages subject to recovery in a lawsuit. (It should be noted, however, that this is not a rationale for testing all children in foster care. The agency will be held accountable only for not revealing HIV information actually known to it.) Finally, although the law is unclear, the adoptive parents may seek to set aside the adoption upon learning of the child's health condition.

Confidentiality and Disclosure

> An HIV-positive and symptomatic parent and her HIV-positive, symptomatic 18-month-old child are receiving services from a child welfare agency. The mother and child have moved into a household with nonrelated adults who occasionally assume caregiving responsibilities for the child. Also living in the household are the two preschool children of the mother's friends/roommates. This mother does not want to share information about her own or her child's health status with the other members of this household, yet she relies on them for child care.

> The MDT medical consultant and social worker met with the mother, discussed her concern about disclosure to her roommates, and helped her to make the disclosure.

The agency should have a confidentiality policy that applies solely to HIV-related information. It would cover anything likely to identify, directly or indirectly, someone as having been tested for, or actually having, HIV infection, antibodies to HIV, or related infections or illnesses.

The policy should comply with local, state, provincial, and federal laws, and affirm emphatically (1) the client's right to privacy and the agency's obligation to respect the privacy of both child and family, including the confidential maintenance of case records; (2) the need for informed consent to disclose information about HIV status; and (3) a clear definition of who in the agency rightfully needs to know the HIV status of a person served. Need-to-know decisions should be based on direct responsibility or accountability for the optimal care of the client with HIV infection, and should not be a response to the curiosity of others. For example, the foster parent should be told about the HIV status of a child either being considered for placement or already in care, and should be given precise guidelines on respecting confidentiality. The confidentiality policy should identify precisely who is to have access to information about the HIV status of a child, and should be available to the child and the child's biological and foster parents in language they can understand.

The number of personnel who are aware of the child's condition should be kept to a minimum. Determinations of who to inform should be made on a case-by-case basis by the multidisciplinary team, and should consider the age of the child, whether the child (or legal surrogate) has the right to consent to disclosure, his or her needs, and the risk of exposure to possible health hazards and/or behaviors that would put others at risk. The number of persons who have a need to know is minimized when infection control and universal precautions are instituted, practiced, and monitored.

When deciding who needs to know the child's diagnosis, the following criteria should be considered:

- Will disclosing the diagnosis directly benefit the child?

- Will disclosing the diagnosis directly affect the foster parents' and/or social workers' ability to help the child?

- Is there an assurance that the persons receiving the information will themselves respect the child's right to confidentiality of this information?

- Is there a legal requirement to disclose?

When there is uncertainty and/or disagreement about the answers to these questions, the problem should be referred to the MDT.

Some circumstances that affect the way an agency addresses confidentiality pose disclosure dilemmas that can be referred to the MDT. Examples are inadvertent or accidental disclosure, duty-to-warn criteria, passive disclosure, self-disclosure by older children, and malicious disclosure.

Inadvertent or accidental disclosure. Safeguards against carelessness, as in talking about client information in common areas or to a spouse, leaving records on a desk, or leaving computer screens on while away from the work area, should be firmly established in policy and in staff training.

Duty-to-warn criteria. A situation may arise that requires the provider to explore duty to warn. This may result in the provider's having to breach confidentiality. Applying duty-to-warn criteria to HIV infection is controversial. The agency should be aware that the duty to warn others about a person with HIV infection has not yet been sufficiently clarified by case law.

The duty to warn might, at times, supersede confidentiality. In jurisdictions that have recognized the duty-to-warn doctrine, its application is only to situations where the agency staff member has reasonable cause to believe that a specific third party is in imminent danger of contracting HIV. Again, because HIV is not casually contracted, the duty to warn generally will not apply to those who come in casual contact with the HIV-infected person or to cases where the infected person is taking steps to protect the third party.

To make a case-by-case decision about the duty to warn, the following steps should be taken:

- Discuss options with the client and the client's family in accordance with state or provincial law and good casework practice, focusing whenever possible on the client's right to self-determination and his or her responsibility for informing others who need to know about his or her condition;

- Consult with the multidisciplinary team, including a physician; and

- Consult with legal counsel.

In summary, state and provincial laws have covered confidentiality in general and in many cases with specific regard to issues around HIV infection. The general thrust of these laws, as of professional codes of ethics, is toward supporting and protecting confidentiality. This principle is limited only by the duty to warn when serious danger to an identified third party is imminent.

Passive disclosure. The issue of passive disclosure is a difficult one. For example, passive disclosure may occur when foster parents need support to care for a child who is HIV infected. It may occur within the confines of the extended family or a foster parent support group, or when alternate caregivers are in the home. It is unrealistic to believe that foster parents will be able or willing to limit their support network to agency personnel. At the same time, agencies should reinforce the primacy of the child's confidentiality. Foster parents and others can use the information on disclosure in this chapter to formulate guidelines that give maximum protection to the child's right to confidentiality. No federal law states clearly whether foster parents have the right to decide who to tell. Agencies should check local laws and regulations for clarification.

Self-disclosure and malicious disclosure. Agencies should be aware that an older child may self-disclose, or there may be instances when an individual maliciously discloses information about the HIV status of another person. These situations should be brought to the attention of the MDT.

Permanency Planning

> Ms. S. is an HIV-infected former prostitute and IV drug abuser, just released from jail. She is anxious to have her youngest son, two-year-old Kevin, returned to her. Kevin has been in foster care for six months. He has AIDS and requires frequent medical visits and a strict home care regimen, including doses of AZT every six hours. Kevin's foster mother, an older, maternal woman whom the mother has met and liked, is able to cope with these special needs. To complicate matters, the biological mother is both intellectually limited and experiencing HIV-related early dementia. Her extended family is already burdened with an array of health and legal problems and cannot care for Kevin. The family worries that the boy, who was removed from Ms. S. because of medical neglect, will not make a successful return home.

When children are placed in foster care, the agency is legally responsible to plan for their future care. Options typically are (1) working on returning the child to biological parents; (2) identifying appropriate kinship care placements; (3) preparing for termination of parental rights and child adoption; or (4) preparing older children for living independently. This perspective also applies to children with HIV infection, but may be complicated by the health status of the parent and/or child and by the heavier caregiving demands of a chronically ill child.

Permanency planning should begin before children are placed in foster care. It is defined as placement of a child in a family that intends to provide the child with a lifelong relationship that includes continuity, commitment, and social status [Maluccio 1989]. Legal status is also an important part of the equation. Permanency planning principles should include the following:

- Strengths/needs assessment of the biological parents' potential for parenting, including co-parenting, which allows for biological parents who are sick or incapacitated to participate as much as possible with the foster parent in the care of the child;

- The role and resources of the extended family or non-kin family members (kinship care) as regular caregivers or as temporary caregivers (e.g., providers of baby-sitting and respite care); and

- Active consideration of the child's cultural and ethnic heritage from the beginning, including the initial placement, with every reasonable effort toward permanency with a family that shares the same culture and language.

Permanency planning for the child with HIV infection or the child who is possibly HIV infected is not a short-term process. Current knowledge about infants who are HIV antibody positive indicates that 60% to 75% will become HIV negative and, one hopes, will be free of the virus. For children who remain HIV positive, and thus, are infected, advances in medical care significantly improve the quality of life and may extend its length. Therefore, permanency planning for the child who is, or may be, HIV infected is a vital and important function of the agency. Because of the dramatic and sudden changes that can occur in the health status of the child, this responsibility requires frequent and routine administrative reviews of the permanency plan.

The Biological Family

The optimal place for a child to grow up is in a family, preferably the biological family. The federally mandated requirement of P.L. 96-272, that the child welfare agency use "reasonable efforts" to keep families together, is not waived by positive HIV status. Thus the child welfare agency must try, wherever appropriate, to provide services to the family that will keep the child at home. These might include, for example, homemaker services that enable a parent with HIV infection to take care of his or her child, transportation services that help the parent attend to the child's medical needs, and respite care to relieve the parent of the constant burden of taking care of a chronically ill child.

For children who are HIV infected, remaining with their own family is not always possible. Parents may be unable or unwilling to care for the child at home. This may be due to severe illness of the parent(s) with HIV infection or AIDS. In situations where the ill parent is incapacitated and living in a household with other individuals who are capable of caring for the child, the ability and willingness of these individuals to care for the child should be assessed. In cases where the child cannot remain with his or her family, providers making permanency plans for family foster care should consider placements first in the kinship care family, then in a family foster home. Visits between the biological parent and the child in family foster care are encouraged in order to maintain this connection in the child's life.

The Adoptive Family

Adoptive families have the same needs for information, education, and supports as foster families. Agencies must know the jurisdictional requirements because the foster care agency has current and ongoing obligations to adoptive families.

> Five years after adoption was legalized for a set of twins, the foster care agency learned that the biological mother, a long-time drug user, had AIDS. Two children still living with her were tested for HIV. One child was positive and exhibiting symptoms. The twins were then living out of state. The foster care agency was advised by its pediatric HIV medical consultant that the twins should also be tested for HIV. The foster care agency located the adoptive family. A medical consultant talked to them about the potential risk to the adopted children, enabling the family to make an informed decision. The family was linked to local medical and social service resources.

Group Care

In those instances where the child's or youth's emotional status indicates the need for group care and/or treatment, see the CWLA publication *Serving HIV-Infected Children, Youths, and their Families: A Guide for Residential Group Care Providers.*

Funding and Services

Funding and services in permanency planning should follow the child. Regardless of the placement, and in addition to medical and treatment services, the child and the parents caring for the child should have ongoing support services as appropriate:

- Case management,
- Homemaker services,
- Home health care,
- Respite care,
- Physical therapy and speech therapy,
- Family support groups,
- Programs for the developmentally disabled,
- Transportation,

- Access to a family day care home or specialized day care center,

- Dental care,

- Financial support,

- Volunteer services,

- Specialized or adapted infant stimulation programs, and

- Hospice care.

Permanency planning for the child with HIV infection requires creative use of financial resources such as:

- Medicaid and Medicaid-model waiver programs,

- Social Security survivor benefits,

- Supplemental Security income,

- Private insurance,

- Community-based AIDS service organizations,

- Indian Child Welfare Act benefits,

- Military dependent allowances,

- Mental health funds, and

- Supplemental Assistance for Women, Infants, and Children (WIC).

Issues Specific to Adolescents

> Tynesha acquired HIV infection when she was 13 after being sexually abused by her stepfather, a drug user with AIDS. Her mother has since died from AIDS and Ty lives with her maternal aunt. She receives regular medical care, including AZT, and has only mild symptoms. She attends school regularly, where she plays in the band, dates, and is involved in many social activities, including a teen AIDS support group. The school knows her diagnosis and the school nurse makes sure she takes her AZT at lunch. Ty is receiving counseling in relation to the sexual abuse, the loss of her mother, and her illness and need for medical care.

Older children, adolescents, and youths (age six to 21) require special consideration. They are of an age to participate in discussions and decisions about themselves and HIV infection. Youths as young as 12 (depending on local laws) may have the right to consent to treatments, tests, and disclosures of information about themselves.

Many of the services required by these young people are the same as those afforded to adults infected with HIV. In addition to individual therapy, they may need supportive group services offered by the agency or by other AIDS groups in the community. None should be denied the growth experience of school and school activities. Prevention education and behavior change are essential to reduce the possible spread of the virus. Constant evaluation of their physical condition and mental health is required.

Children and youths with other serious or terminal conditions benefit from self-help support groups, and there is no reason why a child or youth who is HIV infected cannot receive similar benefits from groups.

Older children, adolescents, and youths will most likely require the following support services:

- Age-appropriate education regarding HIV infection, to increase their sensitivity and to teach precautions that will prevent them from contracting or spreading the virus.

- Age-appropriate counseling and support services for those in family foster care whose parents are HIV infected.

- Education for ongoing self-observation by those in family foster care who are infected, as well as for observation by staff members and foster parents regarding the progression of HIV infection. This education should alert young people to changes in behavioral and neurological functioning, as well as medical symptoms.

- Enhanced supports for those who are infected and for the foster parents as the infection progresses.

- Regular re-evaluation of the medical and behavioral changes in youths who are HIV infected (because their condition may change dramatically as the disease progresses).

- Backup out-of-home care for serious episodes of illness (hospital, group care, hospice).

- Specific kinds of support groups and forms of therapy to meet the needs of these young people with HIV infection or those who are not infected, but have family members with HIV infection. Sexuality, dying and death, loss and mourning are examples of issues that might be raised.

- Education about testing, about confidentiality and its ramifications, and about who owns the information and has the right to disclose it to others.

- Adolescents who are pregnant should have appropriate education about HIV infection as early as possible in the pregnancy, covering risk behaviors, transmission of HIV, and transmission of the virus to the fetus. The pregnant adolescent should be supported in making informed decisions about the pregnancy, her health, and the health of the expected child.

Recruitment, Selection, Support, and Retention of Foster Families

> Sharone is a 10-month-old girl who was born prematurely weighing two pounds, three ounces. She has been hospitalized since birth. Both parents are intravenous drug users, and both have symptoms of HIV infection. Sharone has had multiple medical complications, including hydrocephalus that required insertion of a shunt and a recent bloodstream infection that required a three-month stay in the hospital nursery. She also has a respiratory distress syndrome, is developmentally delayed, and tests positive for HIV antibodies. Despite her medical problems, she could be cared for in a foster home. The agency is exploring the possibility of a kinship care placement with her maternal aunt. Her caregivers will need careful instruction and support.

To meet an ongoing need for family foster care for children who are HIV positive, agencies need policies that are culturally responsive. The preferred placement should be one consistent with the child's racial, ethnic, and cultural background. This is important for a number of reasons: healthy self-identity, bonded social relationships, spiritual beliefs, dietary preferences, health beliefs, personal care and grooming, and neighborhood and community connections. Policies should also promote the empowerment of foster families; simplify foster parents' access to, and interactions with, social service and health care systems; provide concrete, financial, and psychosocial support to foster families; and encourage their understanding and support of biological parents who may be infected with HIV, ill, or incapacitated, but who still want to participate in parenting as much as possible. Family foster care programs should be available for those children needing intensive, specialized services.

Recruitment

Family foster care recruitment is an essential, ongoing task requiring a variety of techniques and strategies, such as the following:

- Using existing foster families to identify prospective foster families for HIV-positive children;

- Working with churches, synagogues, and religious organizations, as well as other civic and community groups;

- Reaching out to pertinent professional groups through speeches, publications, and networking; and

- Using local media such as television, radio, and newspapers.

To design, coordinate, and carry out these and other creative methods for recruitment, a community-based, community-representative task force could be created. Recruitment initiatives would also be enhanced by:

- Intensifying recruitment efforts in ethnic, linguistic, and racial populations from which many children needing family foster care derive;

- Developing a community-wide interagency clearinghouse for prospective foster parents;

- Recognizing that a significant number of adolescents recruit their own foster families (Ethnic and racial issues may be prominent in this self-recruitment of foster families.), and ensuring that these candidates should receive the same consideration as any other candidate;

- Building flexibility in licensing and certification standards to allow consideration of less restrictive age ranges and family structures;

- Establishing procedures for recruiting kinship care families and foster parents with the same expectations for selection, training, supervision, compensation, and support as nonrelative parents and families; and

- Identifying and replicating successful models and examples of public and private sector communication and coordination in recruitment efforts.

Selection

Recognizing the urgent role of recruitment does not mean compromising the quality of standards in the selection of foster parents. In fact, beyond emphasizing CWLA standards for all foster parents, some criteria should be highlighted in assessments with prospective foster parent applicants for children with HIV:

- Have the applicants demonstrated an ability to deal with HIV infection, chronic illness, and medical issues, and are they willing to give priority to the child's needs? Can they devote time and energy to carrying out the medical plan?

- Do the applicants unduly fear transmission of HIV through casual contact? Are they well informed about HIV and comfortable with showing affection to the child?

- Do the applicants understand the legal requirements concerning confidentiality about the child's diagnosis, and do they accept the responsibility and have the ability to guard this information?

- Have the applicants considered and do they appreciate the significance of HIV disclosure? Have they thought about how to react if a child or youth discloses his or her HIV status? Self-disclosure is not unusual for children and youths. How will the candidates cope, and help the child cope, with the attendant reactions from the community?

- Do the applicants have support systems in place, involving mature individuals who can provide periodic child care, or can such a system be developed?

- Have the applicants considered how other family members might respond if they take a child with HIV? Are they prepared to handle the situation, as parents, if someone in the community finds out about the child's HIV status?

- What are the applicants' motives for foster-parenting a child with HIV?

- What are the applicant's attitudes toward the child's biological parents, and are they willing to maintain contact and involvement with them as specified in a case plan?

- Are the applicants willing to participate responsibly in agency-required activities, such as training; support groups; reporting to, and being under the supervision of, a foster care worker; and medical instructions and planning?

Prospective foster care providers are expected to be actively involved in the child's care, in the monitoring of the child's health and psychosocial status, and in the planning and implementation of plans for the child's well-being.

Agency Support to Foster Parents

> Louis was born prematurely, in a neighborhood with a high incidence of HIV infection, to a woman with a long history of intravenous drug use who had no prenatal care. Because of all these factors, doctors recommended testing the baby. He was found to be HIV positive. At three months of age he was discharged from the hospital and, due to his mother's continued drug use and illness, placed in an agency-approved foster home. The multidisciplinary team (MDT) evaluated Louis' need for services in light of his prematurity and exposure to HIV. He received services through an early intervention program to address his developmental delay, along with regular medical care. By the time he was two, HIV testing showed that he had lost maternal antibodies. He has remained negative in subsequent testings.
>
> This foster mother was employed, but because persons in the community feared HIV, she could not find a baby-sitter. The agency was able to provide the support of a homemaker 40 hours a week so the foster mother could continue working. Louis' mother has since died of AIDS, and his foster mother is considering adopting him.

The agency has a number of expectations of foster parents, but also has obligations of its own, including the duty to support family foster parents appropriately. This support includes the tangible assistance of an enhanced rate of payment for resources that enable the parents to care for the child's needs. This enhanced stipend accords with the difficulty of care and the level of effort required in caring for a chronically ill child. Other important supports include the following:

- Supportive services such as respite care, homemakers, transportation, day care, special cleaning supplies, and clothing;

- Psychosocial support by means of parent support groups, recreational and social activities, mental health services, and agency assistance to foster parents for developing informal psychosocial supports;

- Twenty-four-hour access to a social worker or medical professional knowledgeable about the child and the family;

- Access to a professional within the agency, expert in HIV matters, who serves as a resource to foster parents and casework staff members;

- A system for coordinating and managing services the child is receiving to lessen the stress of dealing with multiple agencies and professionals;

- Active participation in planning of child welfare, social, and medical services;

- Access to a foster family buddy system for ongoing support, providing culturally, racially, and socially responsive experiences;

- Education on how to deal with situations in the community where persons recognize that the foster child is infected with HIV;

- Opportunities for experiences and resources that are culturally and racially sensitive, when cross-cultural placements are necessary;

- Resources to encourage and assist the development of a foster family association;

- Encouragement to participate in educational seminars, including the provision of child care; and

- Assistance with insurance and other financial considerations.

Retention

Agencies with foster families caring for children with HIV have found that retention of foster parents, as well as effective help for the children, depends heavily on an enriched monthly stipend and a range of agency supports, including specialized training and available, responsive foster care workers. Involvement in foster parent support groups and periodic recognition by the agency of the foster parents' contributions (for example, an annual dinner or social event) have also been cited as encouraging and sustaining to foster parents. Veteran foster parents should be encouraged to share their experiences with other foster parents and community groups.

Education and Training

Education and training are the foundations for successful foster care placements. Education is the single most vital strategy for preventing HIV infection. Every child welfare agency should be conducting whatever activities are necessary to educate parents, agency staff members, children and youths, foster parents, and the general community regarding HIV infection. Helping foster parents and staff members understand the cultural, ethnic, and racial issues the child brings to the family foster care placement is another critical educational component.

Education and Training of Foster Parents

The educational content should include up-to-date factual answers to commonly asked questions regarding HIV infection, prevention, transmission, testing, and treatment, as well as a description of agency policies. All forms of communication are educational channels. Materials such as brochures, posters, pamphlets, videos, and films can be made available through mailings, in reception areas, at initial orientations for prospective foster parents, and through agency lending libraries and speakers' bureaus. The information should be supplemented by face-to-face contact and discussion with foster care workers, foster parent educators, or other appropriate staff members. Materials should be understandable, using words that are not too medically complex, and in the readers' first language, if necessary. (See Appendix E for a list of practical reminders for foster families in the care of children with HIV infection.) The approach to education for the kinship care family will have to be adjusted, of course, to respect affectional ties.

Specialized training covers the following content:

- The variability of the disease process in HIV, the unpredictability of its progression over time, and the stress of uncertainty on children and their families;

- Universal precautions and infection control techniques;

- Well-child care and normal development;

- The impact of chronic illness on the child's development, and how to adjust caregiving expectations;

- The psychosocial aspects of caring for a chronically ill child, and the impact on the foster family and the child's biological family;

- The relationship with biological parents as to visiting, co-parenting, and the illness and its progression;

- How to discuss the illness and its ramifications with the affected child and the other children in the home;

- Confidentiality, and identifying who needs to know;

- Working with the health care system—the various specialized services and how to access them—and the role of the primary care physician;

- Working with the social service system to access necessary services;

- Responding effectively to community reactions to HIV;

- Techniques to enhance the growth of the child despite the prospect of the child's ultimate deterioration and death;

- Separation, loss, and bereavement: loss of developmental milestones and separation from the child during hospitalizations, or by death, or even, in some instances, through the child's rejoining his or her family; and

- Empowerment of foster parents to be active participants on the planning and treatment teams for the comprehensive care of the child.

The training faculty should be interdisciplinary and draw from the fields of child welfare and social services, along with health care, pastoral care, mental health, child development, and education. Community expertise in these areas should be reflected. Training should emphasize practical utilization of resources. Presentation of material should be in terminology appropriate to the audience, and the curriculum should in writing, standardized, and based on behavioral learning objectives.

Education and Training of Staff Members

All agency personnel, volunteers, board members, family day care providers, homemakers, respite workers, adoptive parents, community persons, and contract services staff members should receive education regarding HIV infection and the agency's applicable administrative policies.

Staff members working with foster parents of children and youths with HIV infection, or at risk for HIV, should receive specialized ongoing training. Training of foster care staff members and foster parents should be done jointly whenever possible. Training modules should cover the same content listed above for family foster care providers and add the following information as well:

- A decision-making framework regarding testing of clients;

- Confidentiality and disclosure of information within the agency and to outside agencies and individuals;

- Coordination of medical and psychosocial management of children, youths, and families with HIV;

- Types of medical and emotional crisis situations that may be encountered with children, youths, and families with HIV, and provision of and access to services in these situations;

- Liability issues for direct care practitioners, agencies, and boards of directors;

- The advocacy role of staff members; and

- Substantial knowledge and understanding of applicable laws and regulations.

Education of Children and Youths

Children and youths being served by the agency should receive age-appropriate education regarding HIV infection and its prevention. Age-appropriate education about sexuality, sexual activity, and sexual orientation should enable them to protect themselves from becoming infected or infecting others with HIV and other sexually transmitted diseases. This information should routinely and repeatedly be offered in group meetings, individual sessions, pamphlets, other reading material, and films and videos. Healthy decision making and dealing with negative peer pressure, coping with stress and anger, and building self-esteem should be emphasized in a continuing effort to promote positive sexual development and sexuality while describing the dangers of sexually transmitted diseases (STDs), and HIV infection in particular.

In their education programs, family foster care agencies should encourage sexual abstinence in youths as the best defense against STDs and HIV infection, and provide information on safer sexual activities with a partner. At the same time, all children and youths should receive information about condoms, including their proper use, application, removal, and disposal. This instruction should be given by individuals who are knowledgeable, sensitive, comfortable with the material, and aware of the misinformation young people and others are apt to have already acquired.

The composition of the training faculty should draw from various community groups serving adolescents. The use of slightly older youths to help with the education of younger children is meeting with success, particularly in relation to HIV infection. Affective, experiential exercises, role-plays, and discussions are usually more effective than just listening to a lecture when these exercises are incorporated into the overall design of ongoing training that develops practical skills and positive attitudes.

Every effort should be made to assure that the knowledge, values, and skills learned in training are reinforced in everyday practice, with special attention given to how this information can be shared with the biological parents of children in care. This will require the development of outreach efforts to educate families.

Education of the Community

Family foster care agencies can play a vital role in the education of the community about HIV infection and its prevention. An individual agency should tap into an existing network, or develop a network with other agencies and/or groups with similar interests. The network can plan for and provide comprehensive community education, and thus foster the development of supportive health care, social services, and spiritual and pastoral care for the child with HIV infection, the child's family, and other caregivers, including family foster care providers.

The agency should be available for working with the educational system to develop effective education and prevention programs in the elementary and secondary schools. The agency can be a powerful voice in publicizing the message that HIV cannot be transmitted through casual contact in families or in congregate settings such as day care and school.

Personnel Policies

Every child welfare agency must have a strong, clear, and generic personnel policy that conforms to all federal, state, provincial, and local employment laws and ordinances pertaining to handicapping conditions, disabilities, communicable diseases, discrimination, confidentiality, and HIV testing. In the absence of such laws or regulations, legal conventions may exist concerning consent to medical treatment, confidentiality, and access to medical records. The agency should consult legal counsel and incorporate whatever applies into its personnel policies.

A safe work environment for all employees, volunteers, contractors, and board members must be provided by meeting or exceeding federal, state, provincial, and local regulations for employees. Since HIV is not contracted through casual contact, the United States government's Occupational Safety and Health Administration (OSHA) general health requirements can be met by adherence on the part of all staff members to the agency's infection control and universal precautions programs: educating staff members about these programs, using proper infection control procedures, and systematically monitoring compliance. The agency should keep informed of current legal and medical information that may affect its personnel policies and practices.

Personnel policies regarding HIV infection should apply to all aspects of employment and personnel administration, such as hiring, job assignment, opportunities for training and development, salary, benefits, promotion, demotion, layoff, and termination. Pre-employment medical screening may include only those tests allowed by law or regulations. Policies must dictate fair and equal employment opportunities in appropriate positions for all individuals. Further, they must bar discrimination against any otherwise qualified employee or applicant for employment because he or she is known to be HIV infected or perceived to be HIV infected, exhibits risk behavior known to lead to HIV infection, or is assumed to be particularly susceptible because he or she is related to or lives with someone who is HIV infected.

Support services to agency staff caseworkers should include, but not be limited to, the provision of confidential medical case consultation, support groups, and ongoing educational seminars.

Although agency staff members may not refuse services to a child or youth with HIV infection solely because of HIV status, foster parents do have a right to refuse to accept that child for care. However, if recruitment and foster parent training have been carried out in conformity with previous recommendations, refusals will be less likely to occur, since the requirements of demonstrated interest and experience, quality of care, knowledge, and empathy with ill children will have been met.

CHALLENGES TO
FAMILY FOSTER CARE AGENCIES

Child welfare agencies historically have committed themselves to care competently and compassionately for children and families who are without necessary supports and resources. HIV infection challenges that commitment and tests the ability of child welfare services to deliver quality service to children and families. As child welfare agencies, through all their various service providers, serve children with HIV infection and their families, the results of their efforts can and will have an impact on public policy. Child welfare agencies must be advocates as well as providers.

Agencies serving children and families affected by HIV infection face the overall challenge of client access to quality care. Quality care encompasses an integrated and coordinated approach of a number of interrelated and complementary human service disciplines whose practitioners are knowledgeable about, and expertly experienced with, HIV infection. Five major challenges are (1) provision of and access to quality care, (2) attention to issues specific to women, (3) funding of needed services, (4) HIV/AIDS education and prevention, and (5) national advocacy.

Provision of and Access to Quality Care

Quality care for persons affected by a complex illness such as HIV requires the cooperation and collaboration of a range of professionals who are committed to this work and competent to cope with HIV and other serious medical, physical, and social conditions. To meet this requirement it is necessary to have the following services:

- Knowledgeable and well-trained social service and health care providers who are community based and have expertise in HIV infection;

- Development of health care and social service resources that include, among others, inpatient care, outpatient care, home-based care, state-of-the-art medical procedures and equipment, and hospice care;

- Child-development services for infants and young children, such as stimulation programs, and including such disciplines as occupational therapy, physical therapy, and recreational therapy;

- Developmental and enrichment services such as those available in Head Start, preschool programs, day care, and public schools.

Child welfare agencies should use their current resources to emphasize HIV prevention and education and advocate for social services adequate to meet the needs of children with HIV infection and their families. The most humane and vital advocacy is offering caring and supportive services with the limited money available while leading or actively joining in community efforts to establish other needed services—a process that should lead to a definitive continuum-of-care project plan for the community and the HIV-infected families.

The continuum-of-care plan should incorporate the following elements:

- Integrating children or families with HIV infection into existing services for those with special health needs;

- Integrating women who are HIV infected or at risk of infection into existing social and health care programs for those with special needs;

- Providing education and early identification for HIV infection in a proactive manner;

- Developing a community-based network of services offering expertise in HIV infection and an effective referral process with follow-up services;

- Providing child-centered, family-focused, specialized resources with a high level of expertise and knowledge for maximum effectiveness, offered in the least restrictive setting possible; and

- Designing alternative care plans for noninfected children of HIV-infected parents or other caregivers who are too ill to be responsible for children or who have died from AIDS.

Access is key to the provision of quality services in a continuum-of-care plan. Services are useless unless they are accessible to families in need; to be useful they must be community based, easily reached, comprehensive, and especially responsive to the cultures of families. Using the primary language of community members in written materials and employing bilingual service providers both make programs more accessible. So do affordable services, so that families are not denied what they should have.

Issues Specific to Women

The women who are presently at highest risk for HIV infection are inner-city African-American and Latino women. These women have had little or no economic and social power, and have had chronically inadequate access to health care. Many have a deeply rooted cultural orientation to care for others at their own expense, and many are knowingly or unknowingly dependent emotionally and financially upon men who use intravenous drugs.

To have the greatest impact upon women, education and prevention activities must speak to them in gender-specific and culturally relevant terms, emphasizing the risks associated with substance abuse, including IV drug use, and contact with infected partners. Women who are at risk are most often viewed only as purveyors of HIV infection to children, but they must be served by programs oriented to the needs of all women regardless of socioeconomic or reproductive status. The recommendations that follow are adapted from *Generations in Jeopardy—Responding to HIV Infection in Children, Women, and Adolescents in New Jersey.* Education and prevention activities should include:

- Comprehensive treatment (nursing, social work, mental health care) and community-based services for symptomatic women;

- Programs focused on positive behavior and prevention for asymptomatic women;

- Research on the needs and psychology of female IV drug users;

- Gender-specific, culturally relevant education and prevention programs;

- Outreach workers and educational materials at places frequented by women, such as laundromats, housing projects, welfare offices, beauty parlors, waiting rooms of incarceration centers;

- Counseling programs directed to both women and men that will empower women to insist on safer sex guidelines and practices;

- Counseling and support groups for healthy women who are worried;

- Care and service programs for women of childbearing age and for older women; and

- Sensitization to women's needs on the part of health care providers such as emergency room personnel, because this is often the point of entry to the health care system for women who cannot afford private physicians.

Funding of Needed Services

The capacity of the child welfare system to provide the necessary range and quality of services depends upon an expanded funding base. Child welfare agencies should advocate for funds for the counseling, education, prevention, and research efforts; health care training; service provider training; family support services; and other services brought into being by the HIV epidemic. To conserve and effectively use available funds, child welfare agencies must reach out and network within their communities, arranging collaborative efforts and the sharing of specialized resources. Many state agencies have developed effective, specialized family foster care programs for children with HIV infection. The growing number of children who are infected, however, and the fact that many are unknowingly already in regular family foster care or kinship care placements, calls for sharing contractual responsibility with private agencies for the supports necessary to sustain services. This sharing of responsibility would mobilize and maximize precious nongovernmental charitable money in behalf of children and families with HIV infection.

Advocacy for funds should include the following efforts:

- Advocating for funding of kinship care, to include access to the same funding supports to which children with HIV infection placed with a nonrelative are entitled;

- Exploring the funding potential of Title IV-E and Title XX of the Social Security Act; the Alcohol, Drug Abuse and Mental Health Block Grant; the Runaway and Homeless Youth Act; the Abandoned Infants Assistance Act; and other relevant federal sources;

- Inquiring how states currently use Medicaid, particularly the section 2176 waivers (which allow states to provide home- and community-based services to enable individuals to remain in their communities and to facilitate the return of institutionalized individuals to their homes), as a possible source of funding HIV-related programs;

- Working through CWLA and local coalitions, possibly joining with advocates for other catastrophic diseases affecting children and families;

- Encouraging the most effective legislation on HIV infection;

- Advocating that insurance companies, as an ethical obligation, offer insurance for people with HIV infection, while realizing that the major responsibility in this area should fall to the federal government;

- Advocating that funding follow the children and families in whatever alternate care plans they may need; and

- Advocating for funds to be immediately available for all funeral and burial arrangements following the death of a child.

Other challenges continue: prevention, research, testing for HIV infection, confidentiality, discrimination, and civil rights. Education and advocacy around all of these issues will be essential.

Prevention/Education

The prevention of HIV infection is a critical and immediate need that must be faced by policy-makers. Since HIV infection is generally contracted through risk behaviors, effective education and intervention aimed at changing these behaviors is the first line of defense.

Child welfare agencies are strongly urged to make advocating for education and prevention programs in all child welfare settings a high priority. These prevention and education initiatives should strive to:

- Reach children and adolescents with age- and developmentally-appropriate education about physical and sexual development and activity, and about sexual orientation;

- Reach out to the populations, cultures, and subcultures with the highest incidence of HIV infection, such as intravenous drug users of childbearing age, their sexual partners, and sexually active youths, including street and homeless youths;

- Evolve a multidisciplinary approach to planning and implementing education;

- Establish goals for changing behaviors, attitudes, and values; and

- Deal with prejudices and misinformation.

Child welfare agencies should advocate on the local, state, provincial, and federal levels to assure that children and families have access to a full range of information on HIV infection. Education regarding prevention of HIV is based on a comprehensive sex education program. As the content of public school sex education programs is largely determined locally, advocacy should take the following forms:

- Local authorities should understand the need for a mandatory comprehensive sex education program that includes prevention of HIV and other STDs.

- The public school system should be recognized as the farthest-reaching and most productive vehicle for education about HIV infection, STDs, and the risk behaviors associated with their transmission.

- Local advocacy efforts should highlight education of children from kindergarten through high school. Lack of education and knowledge places school dropouts—particularly minority and poor children—and women at great risk of HIV infection. For many of these individuals the public school system may provide the only access to this information.

- Preschool and day care, with their parent education outreach, must be part of the advocacy focus for the prevention and education of HIV and other STDs.

- Child welfare agencies should engage and cooperate with public school systems in early intervention programs for children and youths.

- Child welfare agencies should promote and cooperate with HIV research programs for children, youths, and women (care and treatment protocols, drug trials and utilization of medications, etc.).

National Advocacy

National coalitions and advocacy activities are required in addition to local efforts. CWLA will continue to participate in national coalitions to advocate at federal and regional levels on behalf of its member agencies and the children and families they serve. Member agencies can facilitate this national drive by providing CWLA with information of the following kinds:

- Observations and demographics on the incidence of HIV infection in the agency's arena;

- Local program efforts and descriptions of creative programs that have been effective and might be replicated, or even less-than-successful ventures from which valuable lessons can be learned;

- Impediments to dealing effectively with local and regional needs;

- Resources that are present or absent for the agency and its coalition of colleagues; and

- Examples of how state and national legislation or regulations have helped or hindered the agency's service delivery efforts.

Advocacy for HIV infection services, quality care, and affordable, effective treatment must be directed to all levels of government—federal, state, provincial, and local. Private financial resources, service agencies, and all service providers within larger agencies should be encouraged to create a coordinated and complementary approach to HIV infection.

CWLA issued a statement regarding child advocacy in 1981. Its opening paragraph is as pertinent today as it was then, when the political climate and the state of the economy in the United States brought about dwindling resources and services for children.

> The League's philosophical position is that the contemporary social agency cannot be simply a service provider. It must also be concerned with the inseparability of general child welfare policies, issues, and principles, and the direction of its own policies, practices, and advocacy in each of these areas. Advocacy assumes an interaction between individuals and the social systems that surround them; the welfare of individuals cannot be isolated from that of the community, so that the attempt to serve one without concern for the other is of little or no avail. It portends a responsibility on the part of the agency (arising from its long and vast experience in serving people) to move from case to cause, and to register concern for those external forces and conditions that inhibit people's ability to function.*

Advocacy is seen as a responsibility of all child welfare agencies, and as such is included in all the CWLA service standards.

---

* Phillips, Maxine. "Statement on Child Advocacy." New York: Child Welfare League of America, 1981.

APPENDIX A

CWLA Task Force on Children and HIV Infection, Subcommittee on Family Foster Care and HIV/AIDS

Chair

Constance M. Ryan
Coordinator, Medical Unit
State of New Jersey, Division of
    Youth and Family Services
1 S. Montgomery Street, CN717
Trenton, NJ 08625

Vice-Chair

Benjamin W. Eide
Consultant
Children's Home Society
    of Washington
2568 N.E. 83rd Street
Seattle, WA 98115

CWLA Staff to Subcommittee

L. Jean Emery
CWLA HIV/AIDS Program Director
Senior Program Analyst
440 First Street, N.W., Suite 310
Washington, DC 20001-2085

Subcommittee Members

Gary Anderson
Associate Professor
Hunter College School of Social Work
City University of New York
129 E. 79th Street
New York, NY 10021

Virginia Anderson, M.D.
1214 79th Street
Brooklyn, NY 11228

Lynn Avery
Director of Staff Homes
Beech Brook
3737 Lander Road
Cleveland, OH 44124

William Brown
Formerly: Executive Director
Sophia Little Home
Cranston, RI
Currently: Program Administrator
Children, Youth and Families
Foster Care
Department of Health and
    Rehabilitative Services
1150 Southwest First Street
Miami, FL 33130

Rebecca Burgess
HIV Project Coordinator
Lutheran Family Services
    in North Carolina
P.O. Box 12083
505 Oberlin Road, #230
Raleigh, NC 27605

Carolyn Burr, R.N., M.S.
Coordinator
National Pediatric HIV Resource
    Center
Children's Hospital of New Jersey
15 S. 9th Street.
Newark, NJ 07107

Elizabeth Kavanaugh
Family and Children's Services
    of Central Maryland, Inc.
204 W. Lanvale Street
Baltimore, MD 21217

Phyllis Gurdin
Leake & Watts Children's Home, Inc.
463 Hawthorne Avenue
Yonkers, NY 10705

Colette Habernicht
Richmond Department
    of Social Services
900 E. Marshall Street
Richmond, VA 23219

Diane Hoffman
9 Youngs Drive
Flemington, NJ 08822

Melva Meade
Formerly: Director of Community
    Services
New England Home for Little Wan-
    derers
850 Boylston Street
Chestnut Hill, MA 02167
*Currently:*Vice President for Program
    Services
Lutheran Social Services of the
    National Capital Area
Washington, DC

Donna C. Pressma
Executive Director
Children's Home Society of New
    Jersey,
Chair, CWLA Task Force on Children
    and HIV Infection
929 Parkside Avenue
Trenton, NJ 08618

Gerri Robinson
Chief of Child Welfare
Resource Development
Social Services Administration (DHR)
311 W. Saratoga Street, Room 551
Baltimore, MD 21201

Cecelia Sudia
Family Service Specialist
Children's Bureau
Department of Health and Human
    Services
P.O. Box 1182
Washington, DC 20013

Legal Consultant

Robert Horowitz
Associate Director
American Bar Association
Center for Children and the Law
1800 M Street, N.W.
Washington, DC 20036

CWLA Staff Consultants

J. Burt Annin
Senior Training Consultant
CWLA Training Institute
Director, HIV/AIDS Training Institutes

Madelyn DeWoody
Director of Legislation
Counsel to the Executive Director

Eileen Mayers Pasztor
Program Director
Family Foster Care

Erica Caplan
Program Assistant

Appendix B

Glosssary*

Acute—Illness exhibiting a rapid onset and a short course with pronounced symptoms.

AIDS (Acquired Immune Deficiency Syndrome)—A severe infection of the immune system caused by the human immunodeficiency virus (HIV), which results in an acquired defect in immune function that reduces the infected person's resistance to opportunistic infections and cancer.

Antibiotic—A soluble substance, derived from a mold or a bacterium, that inhibits the growth of other organisms and is used to combat disease or infection.

Antibody—A protein in the blood produced in response to exposure to specific foreign molecules; antibodies neutralize toxins and interact with other components of the immune system to eliminate infectious microorganisms from the body.

Antigen—A foreign or altered protein that stimulates antibody production.

Antiviral—A substance that attacks a virus and stops or suppresses viral activity.

Assay—A laboratory test designed to determine the amount of a chemical, biological, or pharmacological substance present in the specimen.

---

*Based on Appendix A in Anderson, Gary (ed.), *Courage to Care—Responding to the Crisis of Children with AIDS,* Washington, DC: Child Welfare League of America, 1990: 323-333.

Asymptomatic—Term describing an infection, or phase of infection, without obvious signs or symptoms of disease.

AZT (Azidothymidine)—A synthetic thymidine/deoxythymidine analogue that inhibits HIV. This antiviral medication blocks viral production and slows the clinical course of HIV infection; it may have serious, toxic side effects and lose efficacy over time.

Candidiasis/Candida—A yeast-like infection caused by *Candida albicans*, which affects mucus membranes, the skin, and internal organs, and has become a common problem for immune-depressed people. Such oral infections are called thrush, and exhibit creamy white patches of exudate on inflamed and painful mucosa. Common sites are the mouth, esophagus, nailbeds, axilla, umbilicus, and around the anus. Rarely, the infection may occur systemically and affect the heart and the lining of the brain and spinal cord.

Casual Contact—Refers to day-to-day interactions between HIV-infected individuals and others in the home, school, or workplace; it does not include intimate contact, such as sexual or drug-use interaction, and it implies closer contact than chance passing on a street or sharing a subway car.

Cellular Immune Deficiency—Reduction in the number or ability of T-helper cells in the body's immune system to respond to infectious agents.

Centers for Disease Control (CDC)—A federal health agency, a branch of the United States Department of Health and Human Services, that provides national health and safety guidelines and statistical data on AIDS and other diseases.

Central Nervous System (CNS)—That body system consisting of the brain and spinal cord.

Cofactor—A factor, other than the basic causative agent of a disease, that increases the likelihood of developing that disease; cofactors may include the presence of other microorganisams or of psychosocial elements, such as stress.

Contagious—Term describing disease that can be transmitted by an infectious agent from one person to another. HIV is not contagious during the activities of daily living, but it is contagious during sexual intercourse and intravenous drug use. Using the word *contagious* to describe HIV may be misleading because the word is often used to imply disease transmission from casual or household contact.

Cytomegalovirus (CMV)—This virus is a member of the herpes family. CMV infections may occur without any symptoms in more than half of the population.

Infection may also result in mild flu-like symptoms of aching, fever, mild sore throat, weakness, diarrhea, and enlarged lymph nodes. Severe CMV infections can result in hepatitis, mononucleosis, or pneumonia, especially in immune-suppressed people. CMV is shed in body fluids such as urine, semen, saliva, feces, and sweat. CMV retinitis, an infection of the retina, causes severe visual impairment and blindness. Infection of the brain may cause dementia, and infection of peripheral nerve roots may result in intractable pain.

ELISA—An acronym for enzyme-linked immunosorbent assay, a test used to detect antibodies against HIV in blood samples.

Encephalopathy (also called AIDS dementia [AD], AIDS-dementia syndrome [ADS], and AIDS-dementia complex [ADC])—Although there may be other causes such as herpes simplex, cytomegalovirus, or toxoplasmosis, the most common cause is believed to be direct involvement of the brain by HIV, resulting in sensory disturbance, personality changes, memory and judgment impairment, and/or loss of intellectual, social, or occupational abilities.

Epidemiology—Study of the frequency and distribution of specific diseases.

Full-blown AIDS—Those cases of infection with HIV which meet the Centers for Disease Control's definition of AIDS; that is, opportunistic infection, AIDS-related cancer, wasting, or encephalopathy is present.

Gamma Globulin—A component of blood plasma containing antibodies, given intravenously to children with HIV to boost their bodies' defenses.

Hemophilia—A rare hereditary bleeding disorder leading to spontaneous or traumatic hemorrhage; inherited by males through the maternal X chromosome, resulting in a deficiency in the ability to make one or more blood-clotting proteins (Factor VIII deficiency).

HIV (Human Immunodeficiency Virus)—The name proposed for the causative agency of AIDS by a subcommittee of the International Committee on the Taxonomy of Viruses; sometimes also called ARV (AIDS-related virus), HTLV-III (human T cell lymphotropic virus Type III), or LAV (lymphadenopathy-associated virus), it has a selective affinity for T helper cells. HIV-1 is the first AIDS-related retrovirus identified as the AIDS agent in the United States; a variant, HIV-2 retrovirus, has been identified in Africa.

HIV Wasting Syndrome—A syndrome of profound, involuntary weight loss that appears to be associated with HIV infection.

Immune System—White blood cells that recognize foreign agents or substances, neutralize them, and recall the experience later when confronted with the same challenge.

Immunoglobulin—A protein with antibody activity that, when given to a person who has been exposed to a transmissible agent, may be capable of minimizing the risk of acquiring the disease produced by the agent.

Immunosuppression—The decreased ability to fight infectious disease because of a deficient immune system.

Incubation Period—The time interval between initial exposure to a virus or pathogen and the appearance of the first symptom or sign of infection.

Infection—The state or condition in which the body (or part of it) is invaded by an agent (microorganism or virus) that multiples and produces an injurious effect (active infection).

Intravenous—Into a vein.

IVGG—Intravenous gamma globulin.

Latency—The period of time between contracting a disease and showing the first symptoms. Viruses that are not replicating or producing infectious particles are dormant or latent; immunodeficiency may activate latent viruses.

Lymphadenopathy—Enlarged and/or enlarging, hardening, painful, or otherwise prominent lymph nodes/glands in the neck, armpit, or groin. If continuing for more that three months and in different locations, it is diagnosed as persistent generalized lymphadenopathy (PGL).

Lymphocytes—White blood cells found in lymphoid tissue and blood; originating in bone marrow, they are involved in the immune activity of the body as either T or B lymphocytes.

Lymphocytic Pneumonia (LIP)—A chronic form of pneumonia associated with an increase of the interstitial tissue of the alveolar septa and impairment of oxygenation of red blood cells; also called lymphoid interstitial pneumonia.

Neonatal—Concerning the first 28 days of life after birth.

Opportunistic Diseases or Infections—Diseases caused by common agents that may be frequently present in our bodies or environment, but cause disease only when the immune system becomes depressed; healthy persons with normal immune functions do not get opportunistic infections.

Parenteral Alimentation—The injection of nutriments through subcutaneous, intramuscular, or intravenous routes rather than through the alimentary canal.

Persistent Generalized Lymphadenopathy (PGL)—Chronic, diffuse, non-cancerous lymph node enlargement that has been typically found in those with immune system dysregulation; frequent and persistent bacterial, viral, and fungal infections indicate that full-blown AIDS has occurred.

Pneumocystis Carinii Pneumonia (PCP)—A parasitic infection of the lungs caused by airborne protozoa, present almost everywhere, that are normally destroyed by healthy immune systems; the most common opportunistic infection in AIDS patients. Once PCP has developed, the person is susceptible to recurrences, and the outcome is often fatal. It is frequently treated with sulfamethoxazole/trimethoprim (smz/tmp) or pentamidine isethionate in an aerosol form. These medications may have side effects.

Polymerase Chain Reaction (PCR)—A test that determines the presence of HIV by analyzing the DNA in white blood cells. The PCR test is currently under development, but not yet widely available.

Prophylaxis—Any substance or steps taken to prevent something from happening (for example, vitamins, condoms, vaccines); pentamidine or AZT may be given to asymptomatic patients, for example, to prevent or slow the development of full-blown AIDS.

Retrovirus—A type of virus common in mice but until recently unknown in humans; refers to a large group of RNA viruses that carry reverse transcriptase. The AIDS virus is a retrovirus.

Salmonella Sepsis—The presence in the blood or other tissues of this pathogenic bacterial microorganism or its toxins/poisons.

Seroconversion—The initial development of antibodies specific to a particular antigen.

Seropositive—In the context of HIV, the condition in which antibodies to the virus are found in the blood.

Syndrome—A group of symptoms and signs that, when considered as a whole, constitutes an illness.

T Cells (also called T lymphocytes)—White blood cells formed in the thymus and part of the immune system. The normal ratio of helper T cells to suppressor T cells is about 2:1; this ratio becomes inverted in AIDS patients because the number of helper cells is dramatically decreased.

Thrombocytopenia—A decrease in the number of blood platelets, which have a role in blood coagulation.

Thrush—A common fungus, *Candida albicans*, leads to candidiasis of the mucous membranes of the mouth, characterized by the formation of whitish spots there; often accompanied by fever and gastrointestinal irritation, it may spread to the groin, buttocks, and other parts of the body.

Vaccine—Material composed of an agent or agents that stimulate immunity, thus protecting the body against future infection with that agent.

Virus—An acellular protein, much smaller than a bacterium, that can reproduce only inside a host cell; some viruses cause disease in human beings.

Western Blot Technique—A test that involves the identification of antibodies against specific protein molecules. It is believed to be more specific than the ELISA test in detecting antibodies to HIV in blood samples; it is also more difficult to perform and considerably more expensive. Before an individual is diagnosed as HIV-infected, Western Blot analysis is required as a confirmatory test on samples found to be repeatedly reactive on ELISA tests.

Window Phase—The length of time needed for the body to develop antibodies after exposure to an infectious agent such as HIV; this interval is different from an incubation period and generally occurs one to six months after contact.

APPENDIX C

Case Definition
for Pediatric HIV Infection/AIDS*

Infection is defined by one or more of the following: (1) virus is identified; 2) antibodies are present; (3) symptoms meet CDC's definition of HIV.

Class Definition

P-O   Indeterminate infection: Perinatally exposed infants under 15 months who have antibodies to HIV but are not known to be definitely infected.

P-1   Asymptomatic infection: Children who meet definition of infection but have no signs and symptoms that would lead to classification as P-2.

Subclasses

A   Normal immune function.

B   Abnormal immune function (elevated IgG's lymphopenia, abnormal T cell count).

C   Not tested.

---

*Adapted by the Newark, NJ, Children's Hospital AIDS Program (CHAPS), from the CDC Case Definition for Pediatric Infection/AIDS, *Morbidity and Mortality Weekly Reports* 36, 15 (April 24, 1987).

P-2   Symptomatic infection: Children with abnormal immune functions and symptoms; may be in more than one subclass.

Subclasses

A   Nonspecific findings: Two or more findings for more than 2 months, including fever, failure to thrive, 10% weight loss, hepatomegaly, splenomegaly, parotitis, persistent or recurrent diarrhea (3 or more loose stools/day), lymphadenopathy (nodes measuring at least 0.5 cm in 2 or more sites).

B   Progressive neurologic disease: One or more findings, including loss of milestones or intellectual ability; acquired microcephaly and/or atrophy on CAT scan or MRI; progressive symmetrical motor deficits with 2 or more of: paresis, abnormal tone, pathologic reflexes, ataxia or gait disturbance.

C   Lymphoid interstitial pneumonitis: Histologic diagnosis or chronic pneumonitis with bilateral reticulonodular interstitial infiltrates, with or without hilar lymphadenopathy present on chest x-ray for at least 2 months.

D   Secondary infectious diseases.

Categories

D-1   Includes patients with secondary infectious disease due to one of the specified infectious diseases listed in the CDC surveillance definition for AIDS; pneumocystis carinii pneumonia; chronic crytosporidiosis; disseminated toxoplasmosis with onset after 1 month of age; extra-intestinal strongyloidiasis; chronic isosporiasis; candidiasis (esophageal, bronchial, or pulmonary); extrapulmonary or disseminated mycobacterial infection (any species other than leprae); cytomegalovirus infection with onset after 1 month of age; chronic mucocutaneous or disseminated herpes simplex virus infection with onset after 1 month of age; extrapulmonary or disseminated coccidioidomycosis; nocardiosis; and progressive multifocal leukoencephalopathy.

D-2   Includes patients with unexplained, recurrent, serious bacterial infections (2 or more within a 2-year period) including sepsis meningitis, pneumonia, abscess of an internal organ, and bone/joint infections.

D-3   Includes patients with other infectious diseases, including oral candidiasis persisting for 2 months or more, 2 or more episodes of herpes stomatitis within a year, or multidermatomal or disseminated herpes zoster infection.

Subclass

E   Secondary cancers.

Categories

E-1   Includes patients with the diagnosis of one or more kinds of cancer known to be associated with HIV infection as listed in the surveillance definition of AIDS and indicative of a defect in cell-mediated immunity: Kaposi's sarcoma, B-cell non-Hodgkin's lymphoma, or primary lymphoma of the brain.

E-2   Includes patients with the diagnosis of other malignancies possibly associated with HIV infection.

Subclass

F   Other diseases. Includes children with other conditions possibly due to HIV not listed in the above subclasses, such as: hepatitis, cardiopathy, nephropathy, anemia, thrombocytopenia, and dermatologic diseases.

APPENDIX D

Infection Control*

Infection control procedures limit the occurrence and frequency of illness and promote personal health and a healthy living environment. There are three aspects of infection control: (1) routine infection control; (2) specific infection control; and (3) universal precautions.

Routine Infection Control

Routine infection control measures are really common-sense procedures that almost everyone uses at some time or other to maintain and promote good personal health and healthy environments.

Handwashing

Thorough handwashing with soap and water for at least 15 seconds is the most important defense against the spread of any disease organism. Both children and adults should be ever mindful that frequent and proper handwashing is an obligation they owe to themselves and to others.

Wash hands before: Handling and preparing food, eating, giving and taking medications, taking temperatures.

Wash hands after: Going to the toilet, changing diapers and soiled clothing and linens, handling body fluids or body parts, using disposable gloves (see

---

*Adapted from "Guidelines for Infection Control," Newark, NJ: Babyland Nursery Inc., 1989.

below for discussion on latex gloves), taking temperatures, cleaning living areas or sick rooms, nose blowing, coughing, and sneezing.

Environment

Wash eating utensils, dishes, glasses, pots and pans, and cutting boards in hot soapy water.

Specific Infection Control

Infection control measures are most applicable to congregate care centers such as child day care settings. They are steps taken to prevent the spread of infections from one person to another and to keep the environment free from a variety of infectious agents. The procedures usually involve barriers of some kind such as disposable latex gloves. They also usually include using disinfectants in cleaning. An all-around good household disinfectant is a mixture of one tablespoon of bleach and one quart of water, made fresh daily.

The CDC has removed the following body fluids from its universal precautions list: feces, nasal secretions, sputum, sweat, tears, urine, and vomitus, unless they contain visible blood (*Morbidity and Mortality Weekly Report* 37, 24, June 24, 1988).

General Rules

- Use disposable latex gloves if in contact with body fluids or body wastes containing visible blood.

- Clean surfaces (countertops, tables, floors, etc.) with bleach solution.

- Wipe toys, play equipment, sleeping pads with disinfectant.

- Clean toilets and other bathroom fixtures with disinfectant.

- Air all areas daily by opening screened windows and doors.

- Dispose of soiled diapers and materials used in cleaning as dictated by local health rules.

Universal Precautions

Universal precautions are measures used to keep a barrier between a person and blood. One example is the use of latex gloves. Universal precautions procedures are published by the CDC as accepted methods of preventing the spread of infectious diseases. These precautions are based on the assumption that anyone at any time could unknowingly be exposed to organisms causing infectious disease, with a possible chance of contracting it. The basic rule in universal precautions is that there are no special considerations—treat everyone and everything the same. Using the universal precautions routinely and properly is sufficient to control the spread of infectious diseases.

Practical Reminders for the Care of Children with HIV Infection*

Health Care

Children with HIV infection may have lowered resistance to common and uncommon infections. Infection is what causes most deaths. Extreme cleanliness is of the utmost importance to prevent further infections in these susceptible children.

1. Keep the child's skin clean and intact. Regular bathing, at least once daily, should be a rule. Drying the skin, especially in crevices, is important. If there is a tendency to dryness use ointment or lotion. Keep detergents away; they sometimes cause skin irritations that then could get infected. Use protective oils in sun or extreme cold.

2. Use clean utensils when feeding the child. Avoid placing fingers in the child's mouth. Milk and drinking containers such as bottles, nipples, and cups should be handled carefully. Milk should not stand around unrefrigerated. Utensils should be washed or sterilized promptly. If you must put the child to bed with a bottle, try to make it water. If you must

---

* Based on "A Practical Guide to Caring for Children with AIDS," New Jersey Department of Human Services, Division of Youth and Family Services, 1989.

fill it with milk or juice, be sure to remove it from the child's mouth after one half hour to prevent the growth of bacteria.

3. Eating (particularly sucking and swallowing) can sometimes cause discomfort for infected infants and children. This can interfere with the child's getting enough nourishment to grow properly. You need to be patient and innovative in getting the child to eat.

4. Feed the child a nutritious diet. Avoid junk foods such as potato chips, candy, and cake. Avoid soft drinks. Give fruit juices or milk instead. Remember that milk is both a food and a drink.

5. Watch for sneaky fevers. You should have a rectal thermometer that you use only for that child. It should be cleaned with soap and cold water and placed in a container used only for that thermometer.

6. Be careful with the child's clothes and toys. Frequent washing of clothes and toys, or even boiling if the child has smeared diarrhea movement or vomit, prevents skin infections. Keep your home as clean as possible.

7. Keep the child's nose and face especially clean during colds. Mucus from runny noses can transmit colds. The skin under the nose needs extra care to avoid rawness and infection. If you have a cold, wash your hands more frequently. See that other children and adults do so too.

8. Dispose of soiled diapers in tied plastic bags. Wash your hands carefully before and after changing. Keep gloves available to use if child has diarrhea or vomits.

9. Keep medical appointments. Keep medical records handy. Weight loss is an important symptom. Keep track of it by weighing the child between visits. Remember, injections are different for children with HIV infection; always remind the nurse or doctor before the injection is given.

10. Keep on top of any illness. Report any symptoms promptly to your doctor or nurse. Follow medication directions exactly.

11. Be alert to changes in the child's energy level. No pep is often the first symptom of complications.

12. Be careful with cuts, bruises, and oozing areas. Keep them covered with sterile bandages. Keep blood and pus off your own hands. Wash your hands carefully. Wear gloves, if they make you feel more

comfortable. When blood is smeared on any surface in the home, it should be cleaned with a weak solution of household bleach.

13. Children with HIV infection need stroking and hugging as much as healthy children do. Mouth-to-mouth kissing is not advisable for any child, especially a child with HIV infection who is susceptible to other infections.

Appendix F

Selected Resources on HIV and Acquired Immune Deficiency Syndrome (AIDS)*

Children and Youths

"AIDS, Children, and Child Welfare." A report prepared by Macro Systems, Inc., to the Assistant Secretary for Planning and Evaluation, Department of Health and Human Services, March 31, 1988.

Alger, I. (ed.). "Attention-Deficit Hyperactivity Disorder: AIDS in Children and Adolescents." *Hospital and Community Psychiatry* 40, 12 (December 1989): 1222–23.

Anderson, Gary R. "Children and AIDS: Implications for Child Welfare." *CHILD WELFARE* LXIII, 1 (January–February 1984): 62–73.

Anderson, Gary R. *Children and AIDS: The Challenge for Child Welfare.* Washington, DC: Child Welfare League of America, 1986.

Anderson, Gary R. (ed.). *Courage to Care: Responding to the Crisis of Children with AIDS.* Washington, DC: The Child Welfare League of America, 1990.

Aronson, Susan S. "AIDS and the Child Care Program." *Child Care Information Exchange* 58 (November 1987): 35–39.

Aronson, Susan S. "Ask Dr. Sue: AIDS Policies for Early Childhood Settings." *Child Care Information Exchange* 73 (June 1990): 34–35.

---

*Based on a bibliography prepared by the Child Welfare League of America Information Service, Washington, DC: CWLA,1990.

Boland, Mary G. *The Child with HIV Infection: A Guide for Parents*. Newark, NJ: Children's Hospital of New Jersey, 1986.

Boland, Mary G.; Allen, Theodore J.; Long, Gwendolyn I.; and Tasker, Mary. "Children with HIV Infection: Collaborative Responsibilities of the Child Welfare and Medical Communities." *Social Work* 33, 6 (November–December 1988): 504–509.

Boland, Mary G.; Tasker, Mary; Evans, Patricia M.; and Keresztes, Judith S. "Helping Children with AIDS: The Role of the Child Welfare Worker." *Public Welfare* 45, 1 (Winter 1987): 23–29.

Boland, Mary, and Rizzi, Deborah. *The Child with AIDS: A Guide for Families*. Newark, NJ: Children's Hospital of New Jersey, 1986.

Centers for Disease Control. *HIV/AIDS Surveillance*. Atlanta, GA: CDC, August 1990.

Chachkes, Esther. "Women and Children with AIDS." In *Responding to AIDS: Psychosocial Initiatives*, edited by Carl G. Laukefeld and Manuel Fimbres. Silver Spring, MD: National Association of Social Workers, 1987, 51–64.

Children's Defense Fund. *Teens and AIDS: Opportunities for Prevention*. Washington, DC: CDF, 1988.

Child Welfare League of America. *Attention to AIDS. Proceedings of a Seminar Responding to the Growing Number of Children and Youth with AIDS*. Washington, DC: CWLA,1988.

Child Welfare League of America. The Hugs InVited Series: *Caring for Infants and Toddlers with HIV Infection, Caring for School-Age Children with HIV Infection*, and *Adolescents: At Risk for HIV Infection*. Videos and discussion guides. Washington, DC: Child Welfare League of America, 1991.

Child Welfare League of America. *Report of the CWLA Task Force on Children and HIV Infection. Initial Guidelines*. Washington, DC: Child Welfare League of America, 1988.

Child Welfare League of America. *Serving Children with HIV Infection in Day Care: A Guide for Center-Based and Family Day Care Providers*. Washington, DC: Child Welfare League of America, 1991.

Child Welfare League of America. *Serving HIV-Infected Children, Youth, and Their Families: A Guide for Residential Group Care Providers*. Washington, DC: Child Welfare League of America, 1989.

Child Welfare League of America. *With Loving Arms*. Video and discussion guide developed to assist in recruiting foster parents for HIV-infected children. Washington, DC: Child Welfare League of America, 1989.

Citizens' Committee for Children of New York, Inc. *The Invisible Emergency: Children and AIDS in New York*. New York: Citizens' Committee for Children of New York, Inc., April 1987.

Cooper, Ellen R. "AIDS in Children: An Overview of the Medical, Epidemiological, and Public Health Problems." *New England Journal of Public Policy* 4, 1 (Winter–Spring 1988): 121–134.

Crocker, Allen, and Cohen, Herbert. *Guidelines on Developmental Services for Children and Adults with HIV Infection, Second Edition*. American Association of University-Affiliated

Programs for Persons with Developmental Disabilities, February 1990.

Dardick, Geeta. "For Parents Who Want to Tell Their Children the Facts about AIDS." *Single Parent* 31, 2 (March–April 1988): 17–20, 46.

DiBlasio, Frederick A. "Adolescent Sexuality: Promoting the Search for Hidden Values." *CHILD WELFARE* LXVIII, 3 (May–June 1989): 331–337.

DiClemente, R.J. "Prevention of Human Immunodeficiency Virus Infection among Adolescents: The Interplay of Health Education and Public Policy in the Development and Implementation of School–Based AIDS Education Programs." *AIDS Education and Prevention: An Interdisciplinary Journal* 1, 1 (Spring, 1989): 70–78.

DiClemente, R.J.; Zorn, J.; and Temoshok, L. "Adolescents and AIDS: A Survey of Knowledge, Attitudes, and Beliefs about AIDS in San Francisco." *American Journal of Public Health* 76, 12 (December 1986): 1443–1445.

Fischi, Margaret A., et al. "Evaluation of Heterosexual Partners, Children, and Household Contacts of Adults with AIDS." *Journal of the American Medical Association* 257, 5 (February 6, 1987): 640–644.

Forrest, J.D., and Silverman, J. "What Public School Teachers Teach about Preventing Pregnancy, AIDS, and Sexually Transmitted Diseases. *Family Planning Perspectives* 21, 2 (March/April 1989): 65–72.

Gelber, Seymour. "Developing an AIDS Program in a Juvenile Detention Center." *Children Today* 17, 1 (January–February 1988): 6–9.

Granger, Michele F.; Rosen, Sheri; Yokoyama, Joy; and Tasker, Mary. "Transitional Group Homes for Children with HIV: Support for Children, Families and Foster Parents." *Zero to Three* 9, 3 (February 1989): 14–18.

Gurdin, Phyllis, and Anderson, Gary R. "Quality Care for Ill Children: AIDS-Specialized Foster Family Homes." *Child Welfare* LXVI, 4 (July–August 1987): 291–302.

Hutchings, John J. "Pediatric AIDS: An Overview." *Children Today* 17, 3 (May–June 1988): 4–7.

Kaus, Danek S., and Reed, Robert D. *AIDS: Your Child and the School.* Saratoga, CA: R&E Publishers, 1986.

Kenney, A.M.; Guardado, S.; and Brown, L. "Sex Education and AIDS Education in the Schools: What States and Large School Districts Are Doing." *Family Planning Perspectives* 21, 2 (March–April 1989): 56–64.

Kirp, David L.; with Epstein, Steven; Franks, Marlene Strong; Simon, Jonathan; Conaway, Douglas; and Lewis, John. *Learning by Heart: AIDS and Schoolchildren in American Communities.* New Brunswick, NJ: Rutgers University Press, 1989.

Lewert, George. "Children and AIDS." *Social Casework* 69, 6 (June 1988): 348–354.

Comments from readers on "Children and AIDS." *Social Casework* 69, 12 (December 1988): 644.

Lockhart, Lettie L., and Wodarski, John S. "Facing the Unknown: Children and Adolescents with AIDS." *Social Work* 34, 3 (May 1989): 215–221.

Maluccio, A.N., and Fein, E. "Permanency Planning: A Redefinition." *CHILD WELFARE* LXII, 3 (May/June 1983): 195–201.

Margolis, Stephen; Baughman, Lela; Flynt, J. William; and Kotler, Martin. "AIDS Children and Child Welfare." Report prepared by Macro Systems, Inc., to Assistant Secretary for Planning and Evaluation, U.S. Department of Health and Human Services, 1988.

Miller, Jaclyn, and Carlton, Thomas O. "Children and AIDS: A Need to Rethink Child Welfare Practice." *Social Work* 33, 6 (November–December 1988): 553–555.

National Commission on Acquired Immune Deficiency Syndrome. Annual Report to the President and the Congress. August 1988.

National Commission to Prevent Infant Mortality. *Perinatal AIDS*. Washington, DC: National Center for Health Education, 1987.

National Criminal Justice Reference Service. "Selected Readings on AIDS and Youth." Abstracts from NIJ/NCJRS Collection. Rockville, MD: NCJRS Customer Service, 1987.

New Jersey Department of Human Services. "A Practical Guide to Caring for Children with AIDS." Developed by the Medical Unit; Office of Policy, Planning, and Support; Division of Youth and Family Services; New Jersey Department of Human Services, 1989.

New Jersey Pediatric AIDS Advisory Committee. *Generations in Jeopardy: Responding to HIV Infection in Children, Women, and Adolescents in New Jersey*. Report, September 1989.

Olson, Sydney. "Pediatric HIV: More than a Health Problem." *Children Today* 17, 3 (May–June 1988): 8–9.

Osborne, June E., M.D. "Dispelling Myths about the AIDS Epidemic." Adapted for AIDS Prevention and Services Workshop, Washington, DC, February 15–16, 1990.

Pediatric AIDS Coalition. 1990 Legislative Agenda. Washington, DC, 1990.

Quackenbush, Marcia, and Nelson, Mary, with Clark, Kay (eds.). *The AIDS Challenge: Prevention Education for Young People*. Santa Cruz, CA: Network Publications, 1988.

Quackenbush, Marcia, and Sargent, Pamela. *Teaching AIDS: A Resource Guide on Acquired Immune Deficiency Syndrome*. Santa Cruz, CA: Network Publications, 1986.

Quackenbush, Marcia, and Villarreal, Sylvia. *Does AIDS Hurt? Educating Young Children about AIDS*. Santa Cruz, CA: Network Publications, 1988.

"Questions and Answers about AIDS." *PTA Today* (February 1988).

Raper, Jim, and Aldridge, Jerry. "What Every Teacher Should Know about AIDS." *Childhood Education* 64, 3 (February 1988): 146–149.

Schinke, S.P., Holden, G.W., and Moncher, M.S. "Preventing HIV Infection among Black and Hispanic Adolescents." *Journal of Social Work and Human Sexuality* 8, 1 (1989): 63–73.

Scott, Gwendolyn B., et al. "Mothers of Infants with the Acquired Immunodeficiency Syndrome." *Journal of the American Medical Association* 285, 3 (January 18, 1985): 363–366.

Select Committee on Children, Youth, and Families. "Continuing Jeopardy: Children and AIDS." A Staff Report of the Select Committee on Children, Youth and Families, One Hundredth Congress, Second Session. Washington, DC: U.S. Government Printing Office, 1988.

U.S. Department of Education. *AIDS and the Education of Our Children. A Guide for Parents and Teachers*,1988. Pueblo, CO: Consumer Information Center, Department ED.

U.S. Department of Health and Human Services. Report of the Surgeon General's Workshop on Children with HIV Infection and Their Families. Presented by USDHHS, Public Health Service, Health Resources and Services Administration, Bureau of Health Care Delivery and Assistance, Division of Maternal and Child Health, Rockville, MD, in conjunction with the Children's Hospital of Philadelphia, April 6–9, 1987. (DHS Publication HRS–D–MC 87–1)

Valentich, M., and Gripton, J. "Teaching Children about AIDS." *Journal of Sex Education and Therapy* 15, 2 (Summer 1989): 92–102.

General

American Academy of Pediatrics, Task Force on Pediatric AIDS. "Pediatric Guidelines for Infection Control of Human Immunodeficiency Virus (Acquired Immunodeficiency Virus) in Hospitals, Medical Offices, Schools, and Other Settings." *Pediatrics* 82, 5 (November 1988): 801–807.

American Academy of Pediatrics, Task Force on Pediatric AIDS. "Perinatal Human Immunodeficiency Virus Infection." *Pediatrics* 82, 6 (December 1988): 941–944.

American Academy of Pediatrics, Task Force on Pediatric AIDS. "Infants and Children with Acquired Immunodeficiency Syndrome: Placement in Adoption and Foster Care." *Pediatrics* 83, 4 (April 1989): 609–612.

American Psychologist 43,11 (November 1988). Special Issue: Psychology and AIDS. Arlington, VA: American Psychological Association.

Backinger, C. "Personal Services Workers: A Critical Link in the AIDS Education Chain?" *AIDS Education and Prevention: An Interdisciplinary Journal* 1, 1 (Spring 1989): 31–38.

Bean, J.; Keller, L.; Newburg, C.; and Brown, M. "Methods for the Reeducation of AIDS Social Anxiety and Social Stigma." *AIDS Education and Prevention: An Interdisciplinary Journal* 1, 3 (Fall 1989): 194–221.

Buckingham, Stephan L. "The HIV Antibody Test: Psychosocial Issues." *Social Casework* 68, 7 (September 1987): 387–393.

Buckingham, Stephan L., and Rehms, Susan J. "AIDS and Women at Risk." *Health and Social Work* 12, 1 (Winter 1987): 5–11.

Buckingham, Stephan L., and Van Gorp, Wilfred G. "Essential Knowledge about AIDS Dementia." *Social Work* 33, 2 (March–April 1988): 112–115.

Buckingham, Stephan L. (ed.). "AIDS: Bridging the Gap between Information and Practice." *Social Casework* 69, 6 (June 1988): entire volume.

Centers for Disease Control." HIV Prevalence Estimates and AIDS Case Projections for the United States: Report based upon a workshop." *Morbidity and Mortality Weekly Reports (MMWR)* 39, RR–16 (November 30, 1990).

Centers for Disease Control. *Morbidity and Mortality Weekly Reports (MMWR)*. Atlanta, GA: USDHHS, Public Health Service: Vol. 31, 43 (November 5, 1982); Vol. 34, 34 (August 30, 1985); Vol. 35, 5 (February 7, 1986); Vol. 35, 38 (September 26, 1986); Vol. 36, 15 (April 24, 1987).

Cleveland, Peggy H., and Davenport, Joseph III. "AIDS: A Growing Problem for Rural Communities." *Human Services in the Rural Environment* 13, 1 (Summer 1989): 23–29.

Corless, Inge B., and Pittman–Lindeman, Mary. (eds.) *AIDS: Principles, Practices, and Politics.* New York, NY: Hemisphere Publishing Corporation, 1988.

De La Cancela, V. "Minority AIDS Prevention: Moving Beyond Cultural Perspectives Toward Sociopolitical Empowerment." *AIDS Education and Prevention: An Interdisciplinary Journal* 1, 2 (Summer 1989): 141–53.

Dhooper, Surjit Singh, and Royse, David D. "Rural Attitudes about AIDS: A Statewide Survey." *Human Services in the Rural Environment* 13, 1 (Summer 1989): 17–22.

Donovan, Patricia. "AIDS and Family Planning Clinics: Confronting the Crisis." *Family Planning Perspectives* 19, 3 (May–June 1987): 111–114, 138.

Freudenberg, N.; Lee, J.; and Silver, D. "How Black and Latino Community Organizations Respond to the AIDS Epidemic: A Case Study in One New York City Neighborhood." *AIDS Education and Prevention: An Interdisciplinary Journal* 1, 1 (Spring 1989): 12–21.

Froner, G., and Powniak, S. "The Health Outreach Team: Taking AIDS Education and Healthcare to the Streets." *AIDS Education and Prevention: An Interdisciplinary Journal* 1, 2 (Summer 1989): 105–18.

Honey, Ellen. "AIDS and the Inner City: Critical Issues." *Social Casework* 69, 6 (June 1988): 365–370.

Intergovernmental Health Policy Project (IHPP). *AIDS: A Public Health Challenge: State Issues, Policies, and Programs. Vol. 1: Assessing the Problem. Vol. 2: Managing and Financing the Problem. Vol. 3: Resource Guide.* Washington, DC: IHPP, The George Washington University, 1987.

Kaspar, B. "Workmen and AIDS: A Psycho–Social Perspective." *Affilia: Journal of Women and Social Work* 4, 4 (Winter 1989): 7–22.

Kissel, Stanley J. "AIDS and the Contagion of Fear." *Health and Social Work* 11, 1 (Winter 1986): 66–68.

Krieger, Nancy, and Appleman, Rose. *The Politics of AIDS.* Oakland, CA: Frontline Pamphlets, 1986.

Lamb, George A., and Liebling, Linette G. "The Role of Education in AIDS Prevention." *New England Journal of Public Policy* 4, 1 (Winter–Spring 1988): 315–322.

Lester, Bonnie. *Women and AIDS: A Practical Guide for Those Who Help Others.* New York, NY: Crossroad/Continuum, 1988.

Lopez, Diego, and Getzel, George S. "Strategies for Volunteers Caring for Persons with AIDS." *Social Casework* 68, 1 (January 1987): 47–53.

Luehrs, John; Orlebeke, Evagren; and Merlis, Mark. "AIDS and Medicaid: The Role of Medicaid in Treating Those with AIDS." *Public Welfare* 44, 3 (Summer 1986): 20–28.

Macklin, Eleanor (ed.). *AIDS and Families.* New York, NY: The Haworth Press, Inc., 1989.

Mays, Vickie; Albee, George W.; and Schneider, Stanley F. (eds.). "The Primary Prevention of AIDS: Psychological Approaches." *Primary Prevention of Psychopathology, Vol. 13.* Newbury Park, CA: Sage Publications, Inc., 1989.

McCormack, Thomas P. *The AIDS Benefits Handbook: Everything You Need to Know to Get Social Security, Welfare, Medicaid, Medicare, Food Stamps, Housing, Drugs.* New Haven, CT: Yale University Press, 1990.

Miller, David. *Living with AIDS and HIV.* London, England, and Dobbs Ferry, NY: Macmillan/ Sheridan House, 1987.

Moynihan, Rosemary; Christ, Grace; and Silver, Les Gallo. "AIDS and Terminal Illness." *Social Casework* 69, 6 (June 1988): 380–388.

National Commission on Acquired Immune Deficiency Syndrome. Annual Report to the President and the Congress, August 1990.

National Center for Health Education. *HealthLink* 3, 3 (December 1987). Special Issue on AIDS Education. New York: National Center for Health Education, 30 East 29th Street.

New York State Department of Social Services. *AIDS Resource Manual,* January 1987. Available from New York State Department of Social Services, 40 North Pearl Street, Albany, N.Y. 12243.

Nichols, E.K. *Mobilizing Against AIDS.* Cambridge, MA: Harvard University Press, 1989.

Richardson, Diane. *Women and AIDS.* New York, NY: Methuen, Inc., 1988.

Rogers, Martha F. "Lack of Transmission of Human Immunodeficiency Virus from Infected Children to Their Household Contacts." *Pediatrics* 85, 2 (February 1990).

Rounds, Kathleen A. "AIDS in Rural Areas: Challenges to Providing Care." *Social Work* 33, 3 (May–June 1988): 257–261.

Shilts, Randy. *And the Band Played On.* New York, NY: St. Martin's Press, 1987.

Siegel, Larry (ed.). *AIDS and Substance Abuse.* New York, NY: The Haworth Press, Inc., 1988.

Solomon, Jeffrey R. "AIDS: A Jewish Communal Challenge for the 90s." *Journal of Jewish Communal Service* 65, 1 (Fall 1988): 46–51.

Legal/Ethical

American Bar Association. Policy on AIDS and the Criminal Justice System. Chicago, IL: Criminal Justice Section, American Bar Association, 1989.

Lloyd, David W. "Legal Issues for Child Welfare Agencies in Policy Development regarding HIV Infection and AIDS in Children." *Children's Legal Rights Journal* 8, 2 (Spring 1987): 8–11.

Social Work Practice/Human Services

AIDS: Helping Families to Cope. A Report. Excerpts from the 1987 National Association of Social Workers (NASW) Annual Conference presentations to the National Institutes of Mental Health. Silver Spring, MD: NASW, 1988.

Andersen, Heather, and Civic, Diane. "Psychosocial Issues in Rural AIDS Care." *Human Services in the Rural Environment* 13, 1 (Summer 1989): 11–16.

Buckingham, Stephan L. "The HIV Antibody Test: Psychosocial Issues." *Social Casework* 68, 7 (September 1987): 387–393.

Buckingham, Stephan L., and Van Gorp, Wilfred G. "AIDS-Dementia Complex: Implications for Practice." *Social Casework* 69, 6 (June 1988): 371–375.

Buckingham, Stephan L., and Van Gorp, Wilfred G. "Essential Knowledge about AIDS Dementia." *Social Work* 33, 2 (March–April 1988): 112–115.

Coomer, C.M. "AIDS in Schools: Avoiding a Crisis." *Social Work in Education* 11, 1 (Fall 1988): 64–67.

Corless, Inge B., and Pittman–Lindeman, Mary (eds.). *AIDS: Principles, Practices, and Politics.* New York, NY: Hemisphere Publishing Corporation, 1988.

Dane, Barbara Oberhofer. "New Beginnings for AIDS Patients." *Social Casework* 70, 5 (May 1989): 305–309.

Dunkel, Joan, and Hatfield, Shellie. "Countertransference Issues in Working with Persons with AIDS." *Social Work* 31, 2 (March–April 1986): 114–117.

Gambe, Richard, and Getzel, George S. "Group Work with Gay Men with AIDS." *Social Casework* 70, 3 (March 1989): 172–179.

Getzel, George S., and Mahony, K.F. "Confronting Human Finitude: Groupwork with People with AIDS." *Groupwork* 2, 2 (1989): 95–107.

Haney, Patrick. "Providing Empowerment to the Person with AIDS." *Social Work* 33, 3 (May–June 1988): 251–253.

Kelly, James, and Sykes, Pamelia. "Helping the Helpers: A Support Group for Family Members of Persons with AIDS." *Social Work* 34, 3 (May 1989): 239–242.

Knox, M.D.; Dow, M.G.; and Cotton, D.A. "Mental Health Care Providers: The Need For AIDS Education." *AIDS Education and Prevention: An Interdisciplinary Journal* 1, 4 (Winter 1989): 285–90.

Krieger, Irwin. "An Approach to Coping with Anxiety about AIDS." *Social Work* 33, 3 (May–June 1988): 263–264.

Leukefeld, Carl G., and Fimbres, Manuel. *Responding to AIDS: Psychosocial Initiatives.* Silver Spring, MD: National Association of Social Workers, 1987.

Lopez, Diego, and Getzel, George S. "Strategies for Volunteers Caring for Persons with AIDS." *Social Casework* 68, 1 (January 1987): 47–53.

Macks, Judy. "Women and AIDS: Countertransference Issues." *Social Casework* 69, 6 (June 1988): 340–347.

Magee, P., and Senizaiz, F.L. "AIDS: A Case Management Approach. The Illinois Experience." *Child and Adolescent Social Work Journal* 4, 3 & 4 (Fall–Winter 1987): 130–141.

Magura, Stephen; Shapiro, Janet L.; Grossman, Joel I.; and Lipton, Douglas S. "Education/ Support Groups for AIDS Prevention with At–Risk Clients." *Social Casework* 70, 1 (January 1989): 10–20.

Martin, M.L., and Henry–Feeney, J. "Clinical Services to Persons With AIDS: The Parallel Nature of the Client and Worker Process." *Clinical Social Work Journal* 17, 4 (Winter 1989): 337–49.

Napoleone, Sandra. "Inpatient Care of Persons with AIDS." *Social Casework* 69, 6 (June 1988): 376–379.

Nieto, Daniel S. "AIDS and the Rural Family: Some Systems Considerations and Intervention Implications for the Human Services Practitioner." *Human Services in the Rural Environment* 13, 1 (Summer 1989): 34–38.

Rose, Andrew. "Jewish Agency Services to People with AIDS and Their Families." *Journal of Jewish Communal Services* 64, 1 (Fall 1987): 52–55.

Ryan, Caitlin C. "The Social and Clinical Challenges of AIDS." *Smith College Studies in Social Work* 59, 1 (November 1988): 3–20.

Shernoff, Michael. "Integrating Safer-Sex Counseling into Social Work Practice." *Social Casework* 69, 6 (June 1988): 334–339.

Shernoff, M. "Why Every Social Worker Should Be Challenged by AIDS." *Social Work* 35, 1 (January 1990): 5–8.

Sonsel, George E.; Paradise, Frank; and Stroup, Stephen. "Case-Management Practice in an AIDS Service Organization." *Social Casework* 69, 6 (June 1988): 388–392.

Strange, Rosemary Winder. "AIDS: Ministering to the Dying." *Charities USA* 13, 3 (March 1986): 5–8.

Treatment Programs. "How One Agency Handles AIDS." *Caring* 3, 4 (Fall 1987): 17, 20–21.

Wiener, Lori S. "Helping Clients with AIDS: The Role of the Worker." *Public Welfare* 44, 4 (Fall 1986): 38–41.

Wiener, Lori S., and Siegel, K. "Social Workers' Comfort in Providing Services to AIDS Patients." *Social Work* 35, 1 (Jan. 1990): 18–25.

Woodruff, Geneva; Sterzin, Elaine Durkot; and Hanson, Christopher. "Serving Drug–Involved Families with HIV Infection in the Community: A Case Report." *Zero to Three* 9, 5 (June 1989): 12–17.